MENTAL HEALTH 101

FOR TEENS

The Practical Guide to Mental Health, Self-Esteem, & Emotional Intelligence

By Tom Thelen, With Dr. Kirleen Neely,
Dr. Kimberley Orsten Hooge, & Dr. Elliott Kagan

© 2023 Character Programs, LLC. All rights reserved.

4th Edition – Published April 25th, 2023

First published on December 11th, 2020

By Tom Thelen. With Dr. Kirleen Neely,

Dr. Kimberley Orsten Hooge, & Dr. Elliott Kagan

Published in Cocoa, Florida, by Character Programs, LLC

Back cover photo image designed by rawpixel.com / Freepik

ISBN-13: 979-8580124957 | ASIN: B08QC3SM45

We're Very Grateful

We (the authors) would like to thank our spouses, children, and all the teens in our lives for supporting us as we wrote *Mental Health 101*. It was a very long journey, and we couldn't have done it without your love and encouragement. You are the unsung heroes of this book!

We'd also like to thank our close friends, students, and coworkers for giving us the real-life experiences necessary to make the book relevant and applicable. Special thanks to Cameron Versluis of EmberlyDigital.com for our website and marketing, and to our contributing writers and editors: Natasha Eckelberger, Casie Thelen, Kelly Burch, and Kaitlin Vogel. Lastly, we'd like to thank Reset Schools for their nonprofit mission of promoting mental health, coping skills, and resiliency. Thank you for showing all of us how to "reset!"

Take the Next Step

https://MentalHealth101.org – Discover our award-winning school curriculum.

https://ResetSchools.org – Partner with our mental health nonprofit.

https://TomThelen.com – Book a live speaking event with Tom Thelen.

https://NeelyCounseling.com – Learn about Dr. Kirleen's counseling center.

https://KimDoesResearch.com – Learn about Dr. OH's research and writing.

https://NoBullyingSchools.com – Use our bullying prevention software & app.

Book Dedication

This book is dedicated to all teenagers, everywhere!
These are the things we wish we would have known at your age.
Hang in there! We believe in you.

- Tom Thelen, Dr. Kirleen, Dr. OH, and Dr. Kagan

Please Remember:

Make sure to talk about the important issues of your life with your **parents or guardians.** For most teens, your parents are the primary trusted adults in your life… even when you're mad at them (which is a normal part of being a teen). And if needed, you can also reach out to a school counselor or to a school psychologist for help.

Save These Emergency Phone Numbers:

988 – Suicide Prevention & Mental Health Crisis Lifeline (available 24/7)

911 – Medical & Public Safety Emergency Number (available 24/7)

211 – Health & Human Services Support Line

TABLE OF CONTENTS

Chapter 1
MEET THE AUTHORS

1.1 – Meet Tom Thelen

Hey everybody, Tom Thelen here. If I could go back in time to talk with my younger self, I would hand myself the book you're about to read, and say:

"Greetings Teen Tom. **It is I... Future Tom,** from the future! I'm here to tell you to **hang in there. You're gonna make it.** Now, take this book and devour every page. Don't literally eat the book. But seriously... read it! This book will help you. It will change your life. You'll realize you've always been "good-enough." You'll stop trying so hard to be the funny guy. You'll have better relationships, even romance, and you'll be physically and mentally healthy. With this book, you have two choices: **1)** You can take it lightly and learn the skills over the next twenty-plus years, like I did. Or **2) You can take it seriously and get a huge head start on life.** As your future self, I highly recommend the 2nd option. I can't tell you more details about your future, or I'll mess up the whole space-time-continuum, so please... READ THIS BOOK! Also, please... stop parting your hair in the middle. Trust me on that one. Farewell, and I'll see you in the future!"

That is essentially what I'm trying to say to you, the reader. But it's even better than that. I've enlisted three other experts to help write the book: **Dr. Kirleen Neely**, **Dr. Kimberley Orsten Hooge (aka: Dr. OH)**, and **Dr. Elliott Kagan**. These people are my personal friends, and they're also some of the top mental health experts in the world. But please don't misunderstand. Even though we're great friends, it doesn't mean we agree on everything. We have very diverse views on politics and religion (two topics we will <u>not</u> be addressing in this book). We have different backgrounds and upbringings. We live in different parts of the United States. We don't look alike or sound alike, but we all have one clear mission with this book: we're going to give you absolutely everything we have... every insight, every piece of advice, and every skill we wish we had back when we were your age.

We're calling it **Mental Health 101** for a reason. **"101"** is more of a college term, but it sums up the idea. At colleges and universities, the courses are often numbered by the year and the sequence of the course. English 101, for example, is for freshmen (year one), and it's the first class in English. Courses labeled "101" are more of an introduction to a big topic. They give you a basic overview, teach you the core skills, and most importantly, they give you a chance to practice it and even stumble your way through it. As with most things in life, you have to walk before you run.

As a teen, I could have really used a book like **Mental Health 101**. I was the short kid with asthma and allergies. I didn't know why I was being bullied at school or why I was mad at my dad. Back then, I didn't realize I was struggling with anxiety, depression, and self-esteem, so I never asked anyone for help. Then one day, help came to me.

It didn't seem like help at first. It seemed like getting in trouble. I had missed one too many assignments at school, so the principal called a meeting with all my teachers, my parents, and me. We sat down around a big table and each teacher said basically the same thing, **"Tom is a good student at heart, but he gets distracted with all his joking and sarcasm. He has a lot of potential, but he struggles with responsibility, and he misses a lot of homework."** I didn't know what to say. At the end of that meeting, I was put on academic probation. This was my last chance. One more mistake and I'd be kicked out of school.

After the meeting, my English teacher, Mrs. Burdick, asked to talk with me and my parents. She said she saw great potential in me and enjoyed having me in class. (This came as a surprise because she was my strictest teacher and toughest grader.) Then she started talking about the idea of wearing masks. She said we sometimes wear masks to cover up our hurts. It started to become clear she was not talking about Halloween. She spoke softly and patiently, "Tom, underneath that class clown mask, I see a very hurting student… a student who needs help." How could she see through me like that? I didn't need help, I thought… I needed to get out of there! But something kept me from running out of the room. Before I knew it, I was agreeing to get counseling for my mental health. In that moment, I felt a sense of shame and defeat. And at the exact same time… I felt hope.

Mrs. Burdick quickly became my trusted adult – the person I could talk to without feeling judged. She helped me get into counseling, and over the course of time, it dramatically changed my life. Outside of family, Mrs. Burdick played the biggest role in my teenage years. Even after high school, college, marriage, and starting a family, she and her husband Jeff have always been there for me, my wife Casie, and our four kids.

In the summer of 2017, Mrs. Burdick passed away after a long battle with cancer, and it was devastating to everyone who knew her. At her memorial service I got to speak about the impact she made in my life. As I looked out at the crowd, I saw faces of all ages, even former classmates who were now adults like me, and I realized in that moment… each of them had their own story to tell. Mrs. Burdick's impact on our lives never faded away or faded out. In fact, for most of us, it only grew stronger over time. I still take Mrs. Burdick's influence with me whenever I travel to speak at schools and conferences. I share her wisdom in all of my speeches. I'm forever grateful for her investment in my life, and she will always be part of my story. That's the power of a mentor.

1.1 – Discussion Questions

1. As a teen, what are some of the struggles or challenges you're facing?

2. Who are your trusted adults? Who would you talk to if you were going through a tough time? **(By default, it should be your parents or guardians!)** Write the name of **at least one trusted adult below.** Think of adults you see regularly in-person: your parents, guardians, counselors, etc.

   My trusted adults are: _____

3. **Challenge:** If you don't have a trusted adult in your life (someone you can be completely honest with), then I'm challenging you to make a commitment to find one. **Your parents should be your default trusted adults**, and you can also talk to a teacher, a school counselor, or a school psychologist.

More About Tom Thelen

Tom Thelen is the founder of Reset Schools, a nonprofit that partners with K-12 schools to teach mental health skills and resiliency. Since 2012, Tom has spoken at over 800 schools and has been interviewed on NBC, CBS, PBS, and FOX. He is the creator of NoBullyingSchools.com, an evidence-based bullying curriculum with a smartphone app and video lessons on bullying, social skills, and student leadership. Tom is also a Certified Trainer in Youth Mental Health First Aid, a program by the U.S. Department of Behavioral Health. In 2005, Tom graduated from Grace University with a bachelor's of science degree and went on to write three books for students including *Victimproof, Teen Leadership Revolution, and Mental Health 101 For Teens*. He and his wife, Casie, have four children and live in Cocoa Beach, Florida. Learn about Tom's school assembly programs, teacher trainings, and parent programs at https://TomThelen.com.

1.2 – Meet Dr. Kirleen

 What's Up Everybody! My name is Dr. Kirleen Neely, and I'm very excited to connect with you through Mental Health 101 because I truly believe this book could change your life! I know that may sound a little dramatic, but I say this because a book like this would have made an enormous difference to me as a teen, and here's why.

I grew up in a home where I knew I was loved tremendously, but many of the actions, words, and events that occurred left me feeling unworthy. You know, that "not good enough" feeling. Looking back, I realize my family was going through a massive transition, and the stress showed up in short fuses and lots of yelling. Moving from our native country of Trinidad and Tobago in the Caribbean to a small town in Texas was a very stressful time, to say the least. Although that was many years ago, I still remember the painful racial slurs and anti-immigrant words hurled at me and my family.

At school, I was being bullied for having an accent and just for being different. I was a very skinny kid, which led to jokes about my physical appearance. All of these events set me up to have some pretty bad self-esteem issues as a teen. I learned to bottle up my feelings and pretend that I was okay (even when I wasn't). I didn't want anyone to know I was hurting because I thought it was a sign of weakness. Thankfully, I learned that speaking up is one of the bravest things you can do. This book will help you realize that it's okay to ask for help.

By ninth grade, I was honestly flirting with thoughts of how much better it would be if I just didn't wake up in the morning. I didn't have a book like Mental Health 101 to help me understand my feelings, but I did have sports (track and basketball) and academics. I poured myself into the things that made me feel strong, confident, and worthy, and it changed the way I saw myself.

As my confidence grew, I knew in the future I wanted to help other teens deal with their challenges. I stuck to my plan, and eventually it became my career.

Today I work as a mental health therapist, and I've been able to help thousands of people. I hope as we connect through these pages you will read something that reminds you of your worth and value and inspires you to allow your story to be a light for others.

1.2 – Discussion Questions

1. Dr. Kirleen mentioned she needed a book like Mental Health 101 when she was a teen. How do you feel about exploring a book about your mental health?

2. What is one specific thing you hope to get from reading this book? It could be that you want to address something in your life, or that you want more of something, or less of something. What do you want to get out of it?

3. It's always a good idea to have a positive mindset, especially when discussing new or uncomfortable topics. Write down at least one positive mindset goal you hope to keep while reading the book. For example, you could commit to being open-minded or to fully participating in the discussion questions.

More About Dr. Kirleen

Dr. Kirleen Neely holds a PhD in Counselor Education from St. Mary's University. She is a licensed Professional Counselor and an approved Counselor Supervisor. Dr. Kirleen has worked in the mental health field for over twenty years and has been the chief executive officer of Neely Counseling Center since 2001. She currently manages the day-to-day operations of her counseling center and serves as an adjunct professor for St. Mary's University in San Antonio, Texas. Dr. Kirleen spends a large portion of her time writing, teaching, and speaking to audiences of all ages on issues related to self-esteem and anxiety. She is supported by her husband and two beautiful daughters. You can listen to episodes of Dr. Kirleen's popular weekly podcast and learn more about the Neely Counseling Center at https://NeelyCounseling.com.

1.3 – Meet Dr. OH

Hi y'all! I'm Dr. Kimberley Orsten Hooge, but you can call me **Dr. OH**. When I was in high school, they introduced a Psychology course to the list of electives we could take. I remember being halfway through the course and thinking to myself, "Why didn't we get this information sooner? It sure would've made life easier to know these things about myself!"

Let me rewind a little…I was born in Texas but spent the first 8 years of my life in Trinidad, where my dad was working at the time. Trinidad is a small island off the coast of South America. At age 3, my mom put me in kindergarten, which meant I was **two years younger** than everyone else in my grade. At age 8, we moved to Houston, Texas, and at age 9, I entered middle school. It was a rough time for me because I was so different and so unfamiliar with American culture. Everyone at school already had friends they made growing up, so breaking into those social circles was a slow and sometimes painful process, especially since I was so much younger. I spent a lot of time alone, even when I was at school. Social situations started making me nervous. I became very self-conscious and very self-critical. By the time I started high school at age 12, I had already developed depression, anxiety, and a seriously negative body image. The pressure for academic excellence was a strain, and the need for social acceptance was constant. I turned to drugs and sometimes even self-mutilation because those experiences seemed to give me a momentary break from **my truth** (meaning, the reality I was living in).

Today, I can look back and realize there was nothing "wrong" with my truth. Being younger than everyone else is <u>hard</u>. Excruciatingly hard! But no one ever bothered to tell me *why* it was so hard…until that Psychology course. That class taught me how my brain was changing and how important it was to take care of myself physically *and* mentally. I learned about social dynamics. I learned about anxiety and depression and why they happen. I discovered how to cope with my stress and anxiety, and most importantly, where to go for help. ***I learned that my truth was okay***.

If nothing else, I want this book to help you learn that, too. Even if parts of your story seem broken right now, YOU are not broken, and in this book we're going to tell you why.

1.3 – Discussion Questions

1. Take a minute to think about this question. What parts of your life are confusing or frustrating to you right now?

2. In the space below, write down at least one question you have about your life, your brain, or your mental health.

3. What do you want to get out of this book? When you're done with this book, do you want anything to be different in your life? If so, what do you want to be different? Add your goals below.

4. Make a recurring calendar event in your phone. Set a monthly reminder to **Check Progress on MH101 Goals.**

5. As you revisit your goals and check your progress, remember: you can always add more questions and more goals along the way.

More About Dr. OH

Dr. Kimberley Orsten Hooge, aka Dr. OH, received her PhD in Psychology, specializing in Cognitive Neuroscience, from Rice University. She loves research, teaching, and all things brain-related, and works as an independent research consultant. She has co-authored numerous publications on topics such as pediatric brain injury, resilience in at-risk youth, and visual perception. She is an adjunct lecturer for The University of Texas at Dallas, and is passionate about educating others about how the brain works. Dr. OH lives in Houston, Texas, with her IT ninja husband, rambunctious toddler daughter, dog Henry, and cats Gandalf and Koxka. Learn more about her research at https://KimDoesResearch.com.

1.4 – Meet Dr. Kagan

 Hello everyone! I'm Dr. Elliott Kagan, and I'm so excited for what you're about to learn through this book. It's been a long time since I was a teen, and looking back I realize how difficult and important those times were for me. Honestly, I had no idea what I was going through emotionally and how it would impact my life later on as an adult. I grew up in a small suburban town in New Jersey, just outside of metropolitan New York City. I struggled with a lack of confidence and felt alone with my feelings. We didn't talk about feelings in my family, and it wasn't part of the curriculum at school. If you experienced anxiety or depression or negative feelings as a child, the emphasis was on burying or ignoring those emotions, as if expressing emotion was a sign of weakness. So, I did a lot of burying those negative emotions, and I paid a price for that. My emotional distress turned into physical ailments, which can happen, and I was taken to multiple doctors over years to find out what was wrong with me. Finally, my family and I were told that my physical problems were emotionally based, and that I suffered with anxiety and nervousness. That was my first step toward getting help, and over the course of time it made a wonderful difference in my life.

Today, I'm a psychologist helping children and adults recognize their emotions and discover their amazing self-worth. I smile now when I think of the connection between my young life and what I do professionally. Naturally, I want to help young people overcome and master what I had to overcome and master. Of course, everyone's journey is different, and I know it's never easy. At the same time, I hope this book makes it a little easier for you. Mental health is so important, and it needs to be emphasized and talked about. We need to take care of our mental wellness, especially as we go through today's difficult challenges. I hope this book provides you with hope, validation, and real-life skills for your life journey.

1.4 – Discussion Questions

1. When Dr. Kagan talked about your **amazing self-worth**, what do you think he meant by that?

2. How did Dr. Kagan's struggles as a child and teen end up propelling him forward in life?

3. **"At the end of the day people won't remember what you said or did, they will remember how you made them feel."** This is a quote by the incredible Maya Angelou, a poet and civil rights activist. What does the quote mean to you? Why do you think feelings matter so much?

More About Dr. Kagan

Dr. Elliot Kagan earned his PhD from the Ferkauf Graduate School of Psychology at Yeshiva University in New York. As a School Psychologist and a New York State Licensed Psychologist, he specializes in clinical treatment and school-based services. Dr. Kagan worked for many years at Suffern Middle School in New York, where he served as a school psychologist and coordinator for the Olweus Bullying Prevention Program. Since retiring from the school system, he has continued his private practice in counseling and has worked as an independent consultant in the education industry. Dr. Kagan is passionate about finding solutions that support kids, teens, families, educators, and entire school systems.

1.5 – Guidelines for Group Discussion

Below are some ground rules for participating in our discussion questions:

1. Participate at your own comfort level. If you'd rather not answer a question, just say "I pass." (The group should agree to not judge anyone for passing.)

2. Show respect for all people and all opinions… even when you disagree. Use inclusive language that promotes equality, empathy, and understanding.

3. Create a safe space. Listen without judging. Don't assume you know what someone else needs (leave the diagnosing to the mental health professionals).

4. Get help when needed by talking to a trusted adult, such as a parent, guardian, or mental health worker.

5. Acknowledge that each person approaches this book from their own perspective, and no one's point of view is 100% right, 100% of the time.

Chapter 2

WHAT IS MENTAL HEALTH?

2.1 – Mental Health and Wellbeing

 Hey, it's Tom again. Wouldn't it be weird if everyone was embarrassed to eat healthy food? Or what if people felt bad for working out at the gym? What if we made sick people feel ashamed for going to the doctor? That would be a very strange world to live in, right? In the real world, we would never do that. It's absurd. But that's basically what our culture does with mental health. It's called **stigma – having a negative view about something, even when your view is uninformed or based on inaccurate beliefs.**[1] With Mental Health 101, we want to help breakdown that stigma, so teens feel free to discuss their mental health just as freely as they would their physical health.

What is Mental Health?

The old definition of mental health focused on **mental illness**… so if someone had "mental health," it was often seen as a negative thing. Over time, our culture moved beyond that oversimplified view. Today the definition has expanded to include **mental wellbeing**. (I love it when the definition of a word is in the word itself!) Mental wellbeing simply means… being well!

Mental health is the state of our mental, emotional, and social wellbeing.[2] It impacts the core of who we are as humans: our thoughts, feelings, beliefs, behaviors, relationships, and so much more. It influences all areas of our lives: internal, external, home, school, work, and everywhere else. Mental health determines how we see ourselves and how we interact with the people around us. It plays a huge role in how we interpret the past, how we live in the present, and how we envision our futures. We all have mental health, and just like physical health, it's something we need to work on all our lives.[3]

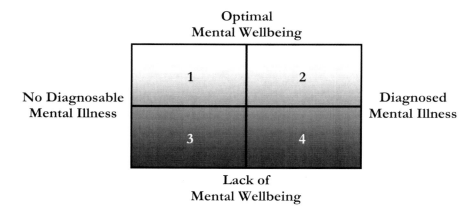

The graphic above shows how **mental wellbeing** is the key to understanding the definition of mental health.[4] (In other words… this is very important!)

Box 1 It might seem obvious, but there are people with **no diagnosable mental illness** who have a very high level of **mental wellbeing.** They strive to live a healthy lifestyle built on positive thoughts, feelings, and actions. They still experience the normal ups and downs of life… the full range of human emotion, but they work hard to keep their mental wellbeing "optimal" or optimized.

Box 2 It might not be obvious, but it's 100% true: there are many people living with a **diagnosed mental illness** (such as major depression or anxiety disorder) **who are <u>also</u> living with a very high level of MENTAL WELLBEING!** Isn't that cool? That means they have the exact same capacity for mental wellbeing as the people in Box 1! Their lives can be 100% fulfilling and rewarding. And why is that? It's because they get treatment from a mental health professional. Perhaps the treatment is in the form of counseling or therapy sessions, or maybe it includes medicine prescribed by a doctor, and we'll talk about all of these things later, but the point is this: <u>these folks are living amazing lives</u>. They are (just like in Box 1) striving to live up to their full potential.

Box 3 This is where I lived for part of my teenage years. I had **no diagnosable mental illness**, but at the same time, I had a huge **lack of mental wellbeing.** I went through seasons of depression. I was anxious. I got in trouble at school and at home. My life was just… blah! It wasn't cool. Listen, if you're living in Box 3, you need to know you're not alone, we don't judge you, and there is a way out. That's what this book is all about: providing you with practical action steps.

Box 4 Sometimes people live with a **diagnosed mental illness** and they also experience a **lack of mental wellbeing.** Perhaps some are unaware that they need help. Or maybe they don't have access to help, or they can't afford it. Sometimes people get help, but the help they get doesn't really… help. Life can be very hard.

Of course, **life is more complex than four little boxes.** Sometimes you may feel in-between, or all over the board… and that's okay. The point of this illustration is to expand our understanding and to reduce the stigma around mental health.

The reality is: some of the most successful teens you know are conquering Algebra, leading a sports team, dating someone, and at the same time, some of them are also battling anxiety, depression, or low self-esteem, and they may not even know it. Our lives are multi-dimensional, and we can't see our own blind spots (that's why they call them "blind spots"). Sometimes we stay in the dark.

That leads us to THE MAIN GOAL OF THIS BOOK: to help you "turn on the light," so you can become more aware of your thoughts, feelings, and behaviors… so you can increase the positive aspects of your life and decrease the negative aspects. No one is perfect. We all have room to grow. My mentor, Mrs. Burdick, used to say, **"You can only change yourself."** That's a good reminder. You work on you, and I'll work on me. Don't waste your mental energy trying to change someone else. As you read this book, I want your primary focus to be taking the next step in your own mental health journey. Sure, you can use what you learn to encourage and help others, but start by becoming a mentally healthy person first, and learn how to go get help when needed. There's no shame in it.

Think about the parallels between mental health and physical health. People who are the most physically fit don't get there by accident. They make physical health part of their daily lifestyle. They eat a healthy diet and go to the gym. They might hire a personal trainer to help them workout. Even when they're not sick, they still go to the doctor for regular checkups. They take vitamins and any necessary medications because they know all of this helps their physical health. It's a stack of healthy choices, repeated over time, which forms a healthy lifestyle and leads to physical fitness. **With mental health,** it's the same thing, and it takes the same level of commitment. But here's the thing: if you've grown up with a lot of **stigma**, it might require even more dedication because you have to retrain your brain to think of mental health as a **VERY POSITIVE** aspect of your life, something never to be ashamed of. As a team of four authors, that's our mission for you. We also have some broader goals for the book. Check out the list below!

The Goals of Mental Health 101

- Improve coping skills for stress and anxiety
- Improve self-esteem and emotional intelligence
- Reduce negative thoughts and destructive decisions
- Reduce mental health stigma

- Develop positive character traits and resiliency

- Develop a culture of respect and civility

- Provide a safe space to discuss mental health and wellbeing

That last goal may be hard to fully achieve, so good news: in the next section, we're giving you a flexible tool called "The Boat Metaphor," a visual aid that helps teens discuss mental health without feeling judged.

2.1 – Discussion Questions

1. Have you ever witnessed the "stigma" around mental health? If so, what did it look like and sound like? Why do you think some people have a negative view toward the topic of mental health?

2. Go back and look at **THE MAIN GOAL OF THIS BOOK** (written in **bold** and ALL CAPS earlier in this section). What is one positive aspect you want to increase in your life? Or if you're brave enough, what is one potentially negative aspect you want to decrease in your life?

3. If you're going through this book in a group setting, what can you do to help provide a safe space for others to discuss their mental health and wellbeing?

4. NOTE. If you or someone you know is struggling, you can always call the **National Lifeline at 988,** and someone will be there to talk with you.

2.2 – The Boat Metaphor

 As a teen, I had a very hard time putting words to my emotions. I didn't even know where to start. What about you? Are you able to discuss your own mental health openly? It can be very difficult to talk about mental health with any level of openness and vulnerability if you don't feel safe. No one wants to be judged.

I'm really pumped about this section because we're giving you a flexible metaphor that helps you conceptualize and discuss mental health. Like all metaphors, it will fall apart if we push it too far, so try not to overthink it.

The Boat Metaphor is merely a tool that helps us zoom out and see the big picture. It is not a one-to-one comparison to real life. Dr. Hugo Alberts developed the Boat Metaphor as a way of connecting with his patients and helping them put words to their complex thoughts and feelings.[5] We hope it does the same for you.

You're the Captain

In the center of the metaphor is a **boat** representing your life. We're using a graphic of a cruise ship, but you can see yourself as any type of boat: speedboat, yacht, pontoon, fishing boat, cargo ship, etc. The type of boat should reflect your personality. This sounds weird, but I think of myself as more of a barge. (Haha!) I may not be the fastest ship, but that's okay with me. I go slow and steady over great distances because I'm trying to bring loads of resources to people. That's the person I want to be. Now, here's the key takeaway about the boat itself: **you're the captain of your own ship!** That means you control most of the aspects of your life. The first seven elements of the metaphor are things **you can control.**

The Boat Metaphor

What you can't control ● What you can control

Steering Wheel
your choices
& values

Periscope
goals, dreams,
life direction

Other Boats
other people

Compass
emotions
& mood

Weather
uncontrollable
circumstances

Fuel
energy level
& capacity

Water
your reality
where you live
& go to school

Lighthouses
Positive influences
& support system

Engine
strengths,
healthy coping

Leak
weaknesses,
ineffective coping

The Steering Wheel represents your choices and values. The choices we make in life reveal what is important to us (aka: our values).[6] When we choose to do something fun, like hang out with our friends, we're showing that we **value** relationships and connection and fun. Even when we do something we don't want to do, like homework, we're displaying our values (maybe the value is: I don't want to get in trouble, and I want to get good grades). It's pretty amazing all the choices we get to make in life!

 The Periscope represents our goals and dreams. It's where we want to go in life. Sometimes we don't even know where we want to go, and perhaps that's why our life feels adrift. We're just floating there. Other times we write down our dreams, and they turn into goals like: learning to play the guitar, buying a nicer skateboard, becoming an inventor, and getting married someday. (Yes, those were some of my goals when I was a teen.)

 The Compass represents our emotions and our mood. Our brains provide all kinds of clues and internal feedback about how we feel about our past, present, and future circumstances.[7] What direction are we heading? If we're doing something we enjoy, the compass point north (so to speak), and we're automatically in a better mood. If someone yells at us, the internal compass says, "This conversation is not going in the right direction!"

 The Fuel Gauge represents our energy level and our capacity to behave the way we want to behave. Do you have enough fuel in the tank, so to speak? When your energy is low, you're more apt to be cranky and say things you regret. Life itself can be very draining, so all of us have to take time to stop and re-fuel. The universe is filled with activities that either drain or energize us. Some of them, like sleep, are built into our biology, and we truly can't live without them.

 The Engine represents our strengths and healthy coping mechanisms.[8] What does that mean? When we're feeling tired or stressed or anxious, we can choose to deal with it in a mentally healthy way. That's called a positive or healthy coping mechanism. We can get our bodies moving and participate in life-giving activities that help us go where we want to go in life. The list is never-ending, but here are a few of my favorites: walking, listening to music, talking with a friend, eating dinner with my family, playing ping-pong, playing guitar, and laughing at the most random things.

The Leak represents our weaknesses and unhealthy coping mechanisms (even ones we are unaware of). Maybe our "boat" is taking on water, and we feel like we're about to sink. There is a leak somewhere, and we need to find it, so we can fix it. We all have leaks because no one is perfect. Sometimes we yell at our friends or family members when we feel stressed. Sometimes we keep eating the chips even when we're full because it somehow makes us feel better. We have to be honest with ourselves and look for the "leaks" in our boat because we know they only bring us down.

 Lighthouses represent the positive influences you choose to have in your life. Lighthouses should primarily be **people,** like your parents or another trusted adult, but they can also be **places** like a youth group or a home, and they can even be **things** like books or documentaries... or even a smartphone app that helps you de-stress. When the night is dark, and the conditions feel dangerous, we all need lighthouses to help light the way, so we can steer through the obstacles of life.

Let's pause for a second. We can control the first seven elements of the Boat Metaphor, so they become our primary responsibilities when it comes to our own mental health. Maybe you're thinking, **"Wait a second! We can't control our mentors!"** And that's true, but don't miss the point. You CAN choose the people you respect and admire... you can choose the people you want to be like. **Next, let's take a look at the last three elements: the things you CAN'T control.** Keep in mind: since they're not your responsibility, they can never be your fault, and that's a very good thing. Even so, having an awareness of the last three elements helps us see the big picture.

 Water represents the larger reality you live in. This includes where you live and go to school. It also includes the social, economic, and political environment around you. Maybe the "boat" of your life feels like it's shaking right now, and you're rocking back and forth in the waves. As a teen, you really can't control where you live, where you go to school, or how much money your parents have. These things are part of your reality, so they make an impact on your mental health.

 Weather represents the uncontrollable circumstances that happen around you. Sometimes it rains, and sometimes it pours. Have you ever had an important activity canceled? Have you ever lost a pet or even a person who was important in your life? Do you always get your favorite teacher in every class? Did your mom lose her job, and now you have to move to a new school? Again, these things are out of your control, so they're never your fault.

Other Boats represent other people and their choices. Stay with me – the point here is not as obvious as you may think. Obviously, you cannot control the actions and attitudes of other people. That said, you do have some control over **who** you hang out with. If anyone in your life is bullying you, or if anyone is hurting, abusing, or neglecting you, you need to report that information to the safe adults in your life right away. And you need to keep asking for help until you get the help you need.

Do me a favor. Go ahead and **bookmark the Boat Metaphor** with scrap paper, or just fold over the top corner of the page. I want you to be able to come back to this illustration throughout the book. Again, it's only a tool – a picture that helps us discuss mental health and wellbeing, and just like any metaphor, it will stop making sense if we push it too far. Lastly, remember that the Boat Metaphor is meant for you to reflect on your own mental health. Please don't try to judge the motives or the mental health of other people. That's not your job. You fix your boat, and I'll fix mine.

2.2 – Discussion Questions

1. Which part of the Boat Metaphor sticks out the most to you, and why?

2. Of the first seven elements (the things you can control), what is one area in your life you feel is a strength (or something you feel good about)?

3. Of the first seven elements, what is one area of your life that might need improvement?

4. Are you going through any difficulties in your life due to one of the last three elements (the things you can't control)? Is there anything you should do about it? Why or why not?

2.3 – Brain Basics

 Hi y'all! It's your friendly neighborhood Dr. OH here. Let's think about our boat some more -why do you suppose that you **can control** the first 7 elements of the boat metaphor, but you **can't control** the other 3? I'll give you a hint – use your brain! *Those first 7 elements are all a product of how your brain works.* Your brain is like your boat's computer because it controls and communicates with every other part of your boat. It steers you through life by helping you to make choices, feel emotions, and dream big dreams. It even sends warning signals and reminds you when you need more fuel. Of course, our brains are still far superior to the world's best computers. But like Tom said, it's only a metaphor, not a one-to-one comparison.

Our brains are critical to everything happening in our bodies, especially mental health. Your brain is an organ just like your heart or your lungs. When something is wrong with your heart or lungs, you become ill. So, when your brain isn't at its best, neither are you. That's why it's important to understand a few basics of your brain, so that you can handle the basics of your mental health.

Neurons

Your brain communicates within itself and with the rest of your body using special cells called **neurons**. There are about *100 billion* neurons in your nervous system. To put that in perspective, if you lined up all of your neurons side-by-side, they would stretch for about 600 miles (that's over 10,500 football fields)! Neurons "talk" to each other by sending electro-chemical signals. The signals start as electrical transmissions that cause a neuron to release chemicals called **neurotransmitters**. Other neurons that are close by pick up these neurotransmitters and pass the signal onward.

Four Lobes of the Brain

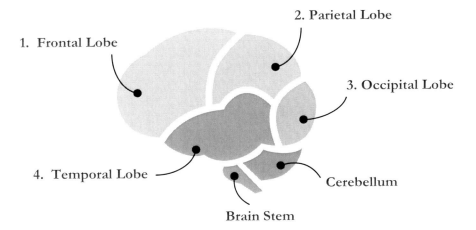

Contrary to the popular myth, we DO NOT "only use 10% of our brains." Every bit of the brain has a purpose. From delivering nutrients, to blood flow, to signal transmission – big things are happening in your brain, and they all play a factor in your mental health.

Your brain is made up of **four areas called lobes**. Each lobe generally takes care of different functions. The **frontal lobe (1)** handles complex cognitive processes – called *executive functions* – like planning, decision-making, impulse control, and social skills. It also handles a lot of your motor skills and some parts of language. It is the last part of the brain to develop as you grow into an adult. Why does that matter? Let's say I put two cookies in front of you and instruct you to eat *only one* of them. And then, let's say I put two cookies in front of my two-year-old daughter and tell her to eat *only one*. Who do you think will be more successful at resisting the urge to grab that second cookie? I'll give you a hint – not my kiddo. That's because your frontal lobe is more developed than hers right now – you are more physically capable of using your brain to control your impulses. But you're not done growing, which means you have your own set of "cookie challenges." Just remember that whether or not you succeed against the challenge, you will always have the chance to learn and grow from it. Your brain cannot make new connections without new experiences.

The **parietal lobe (2)** is involved in taste, touch, pain, and some speech comprehension. The **occipital lobe (3)** takes care of vision. That's right – a whole lobe just for vision. Vision is so incredibly important that our brain makes sure to have lots of room for it. The **temporal lobe (4)** (by your temples) handles smell, hearing, object recognition, and some speech comprehension.

Brain Areas and Functions

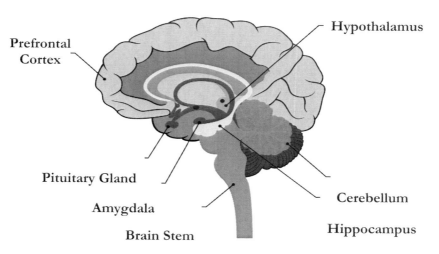

Your brain is also divided into two halves called **hemispheres**. The right hemisphere controls everything going on with the left side of your body, and the left hemisphere controls the right side. There are a few big tasks that are localized to one side or the other. For example, language is usually taken care of in the left hemisphere of your brain. But the right hemisphere can take over if the left side is damaged, because your brain is very good at "rewiring" itself to compensate for damage. It also rewires itself as you learn new things!

You might be thinking, "what's with all the wrinkles?" If you scrunch up a piece of paper, it gets smaller in size. Does that mean you lose any of the information that was written on the paper? No – you just made it more compact.

The wrinkly part of your brain is called the ***cortex***, and it serves the same purpose.

The wrinkles make lots of room for lots of neurons without taking up too much space. Underneath the cortex are areas of the brain that play a huge role in your mental health and physical health.

Here are just a few brain areas and their basic functions…

- **The prefrontal cortex** is the front-most area of the frontal lobe responsible for the executive functions that we mentioned before: planning, decision-making, social savvy, and goal-oriented behavior.

- **The hypothalamus** handles the endocrine (hormone) system by activating the pituitary gland.

- **The cerebellum**, meaning "little brain" in Latin, controls muscle activity to help keep you coordinated and balanced.

- **The hippocampus** handles memory.

- **The brain stem** handles breathing, heartbeat, and certain reflexes such as coughing and sneezing.

- **The amygdala** handles emotions.

- **The pituitary gland** or "master gland" uses hormones to send messages from the hypothalamus to other glands (e.g., thyroid gland).

Of course, there are many more parts of the brain, and it's very rare that only one part is involved in any one function. Neurons connect together to form massive neural networks that link multiple brain areas together. These networks are highly complex, and scientists are still trying to understand how it all works.

As complicated as the brain is, it is clear to see why mental health is also so complex and personal. Everyone is working with a slightly different computer. That's why everyone has different strengths and struggles when it comes to mental health.

Understanding the biology of your brain is a great way to understand yourself and how you interpret the world around you. It also helps us see why we all need to restart our computer from time to time.

2.3 – Discussion Questions

1. Choose an item from one of the 7 elements of the boat metaphor that you'd like to know more about. For example, you could choose "emotions" from the Compass element.

2. Now do a web search for that item, adding the phrase "and the brain." Our example above would become "emotions and the brain." Have a look at some of the results.

3. What did you learn from your search? Is the brain related to the item that you chose? Share your results with someone that chose a different item.

4. Do you think the results you found support the idea that your brain is your boat's control center? Why or why not?

Chapter 2 References

[1] National Council for Behavioral Health. (2016). Mental Health First Aid USA: For Adults Assisting Young People. Sussex Publishers. Positive Psychology. Psychology Today. https://www.psychologytoday.com/us/therapy-types/positive-psychology.

[2] *What is mental health?* What Is Mental Health? | MentalHealth.gov. (2022, February 28). Retrieved May 27, 2022, from https://www.mentalhealth.gov/basics/what-is-mental-health

[3] Giliberti, M. (2018). Improving Mental Health Should Be a National Priority. NAMI. https://www.nami.org/Blogs/From-the-CEO/February-2018/Improving-Mental-Health-Should-Be-a-National-Prior.

[4] *Jack.org Presents: Mental Health 101.* (2019). *YouTube.* Retrieved May 25, 2022, from https://youtu.be/n1z6ddSomRg.

[5] Alberts, H.J.E.M. (2016). The Sailboat. Maastricht: Positive Psychology Program.

[6] Davis, T. (2018, July 12). 39 Core Values-and How to Live by Them. Psychology Today. https://www.psychologytoday.com/us/blog/click-here-happiness/201807/39-core-values-and-how-live-them.

[7] Broadhouse, K. M., Torre, G.-A. A., Eaton, M., & Stevens, H. (2016). Emotions and the Brain – Or How to Master "The Force". Frontiers for Young Minds. https://kids.frontiersin.org/article/10.3389/frym.2016.00016.

[8] Cardillo, J. (2019). Coping. Psychology Today. https://www.psychologytoday.com/us/blog/attention-training/201909/coping.

Chapter 3

SELF-ESTEEM

3.1 – The Key to Healthy Self-Esteem

Hey everybody, Tom Thelen here. As a teen, I only understood **part of the definition** of self-esteem. I thought it only meant having self-confidence in our abilities and achievements, and like most teens, I thought I was doing just fine. Looking back on my teen years, I can see it so clearly now… self-esteem was a huge struggle for me. On a subconscious level, I was covering up my insecurities by projecting a larger-than-life, class clown image. On the outside, I was confident and funny, but on the inside, I was full of self-doubt and sometimes even self-hate (although I didn't know it at the time). I could never live up to my unfair expectation of being perfect all the time, so I lived with a constant fear of failure and rejection.

What is Self-Esteem?

Self-esteem is your overall sense of self-worth. It makes us ask questions like, **"Do I have what it takes?"** and **"Will I ever be good-enough?"**[1] Healthy self-esteem gives us the courage to push ourselves and try new skills, because we know even if we fail, we ourselves are not failures. Low self-esteem, on the other hand, is the voice of doubt in the back of our heads holding us back in life.[2] **The paradox is this: healthy self-esteem is both self-confidence and humility at the same time.** Healthy self-esteem is based on full self-acceptance. It means being confident enough to acknowledge your strengths while remaining humble enough to laugh at some of your weaknesses. The attitude is: *I'm not perfect, and that's okay.* It's part of our essence as human beings: each of us is a work in progress. This is an important lesson I've learned from multiple counselors over the years, and the reality is: I'm still learning it!

When we look at our own shadow (as a metaphor for our self-esteem) we tend to see it one way or the other. Either we see something smaller than we truly are, or we project something larger than real life. Take a look at the shadow metaphor, and notice the similarities between **self-minimizing** and **self-projecting**.

The Shadow Metaphor

Self-Minimizing

Low self-confidence

Defeated perfectionism

"I'm never good enough."

Critical of myself

Blind to my strengths

= Low Self-Esteem

Self-Projecting

High self-confidence

Prideful perfectionism

"I'm the best at everything"

Critical of others

Blind to my weaknesses

= Low Self-Esteem

Self-minimizing shows itself in low self-confidence, so it appears to be the opposite of **self-projecting,** which looks like extremely high self-confidence. In reality, **both are expressions of the same thing: low-self-esteem.**[3] Did you catch that? Sometimes the loudest, most dominant people can struggle with self-esteem issues, even without realizing it. Of course, we should never judge anyone or make assumptions based on their outgoing personality. This is merely a reminder that all personality types can struggle with self-esteem, and it's not always so obvious on the outside.

Healthy self-esteem means being confident enough to acknowledge your strength while being humble enough to laugh at some of your mistakes. The attitude is: ***I'm not perfect, and that's okay!***

Perfectionism & Failure

The question for you is: *how do you see your own shadow?* You can find a big clue in how you respond to mistakes and failures. Notice in the metaphor how **self-minimizing** and **self-projecting** are both built on the lie of **perfectionism** – the subconscious belief that our value depends on being perfect… all the time… in all areas of life. Since perfection can never be fully achieved, it creates internal stress and doubt about our own self-worth. Perfectionism is always just out of reach, like a carrot on a string, and when we fail to grab hold of it, we end up feeling like failures and imposters. Rather than accept our mistakes, we're forced to hide from them or shift the blame to others.

Finding true self-esteem means rejecting the lie of perfectionism, lowering our pride, and accepting our inevitable mistakes and weaknesses. When we no longer have to be perfect, it gives us a sense of lightheartedness and an attitude of grace for ourselves and for the people around us. We don't have to take everything so seriously because we know no one is perfect, everyone farts in class from time to time, everyone poops, it always stinks, and all of this… is just part of life.

What about you? It's easy to talk about self-esteem as a general topic – something a lot of **other people** deal with, but it's difficult to talk about our own struggles. As humans, we are naturally afraid to expose our deepest questions, fears, and vulnerabilities. Sometimes we don't want to know the answers. Discovering the truth is scary, but it's also a tremendously worthwhile pursuit that brings clarity and self-acceptance. In this chapter, I'm challenging you to think deeply and ask tough questions about your own life, because the truth is: we all struggle with self-esteem to varying degrees throughout life, and talking about our struggles is a huge step toward mental health.

3.1. – Discussion Questions

1. What do you think it means to have a healthy level of self-esteem?
2. Is it possible to have high self-confidence and low self-esteem at the same time? Why or why not?

3. Describe the meaning of the shadow metaphor.

4. In this section, Tom indicated how healthy self-esteem helps us not take everything so seriously. What do you think he meant by that?

5. What can you do to have more grace and understanding for yourself and for the people around you?

6. Grab your phone or a new sheet of paper and write one strength you're proud of and one weakness you want to work on in your life.

3.2 – Self-Esteem Triggers and Tools

What's up, guys! It's Dr. Kirleen again. I have been a licensed mental health professional for over 20 years. In that time, I've helped people tackle things like divorce, death, depression, anxiety, and more. But you might be surprised to know the number one issue I see children, teens, and adults struggle with is low self-esteem. Your view of yourself can change the trajectory of your life.[1]

If you're thinking, "It's too late for me" because your self-esteem has been low for a long time, I want you to refuse to give up on yourself. I'm living proof that self-esteem can change. As I shared earlier in the book, I struggled with self-esteem issues as a teen, but with tools and support, my self-esteem is now healthy. Of course, no one is perfect, and sometimes I still struggle, but now I know how to get out of my head and put negative thoughts to rest. So, today I'd like to help you learn how to use some of the same tools that I've seen work in real life for both teens and adults.

Self-Esteem 101

As Tom described, self-esteem is your overall evaluation of yourself, and many times, that self-evaluation gets distorted by perfectionism. If you have low self-esteem, it can lead to allowing people to treat you like a doormat. You may struggle to set boundaries, leading to toxic relationships. The good news is: when you learn how to value yourself, you gravitate towards people who value you, too!

It's crucial to understand self-esteem can fluctuate in different areas of your life. For instance, you may feel super confident about your academics or sports but struggle with how you look physically. You shouldn't look at self-esteem as good or bad, but instead, use words like "healthy" or "unhealthy," and realize you can sometimes have both at the same time.

Envision an apple. A healthy apple may have some bumps or bruises on it, but when you bite into it, it's still delicious. It's still going to give you great nutrition. Self-esteem is the same way. A person with healthy self-esteem is someone who can celebrate their strengths and recognize areas that need improvement. They don't chase perfection, and they know it's okay to show up as 100% themselves.

As a counselor, I know it's common for people to beat themselves up for struggling with self-esteem. Go easy on yourself! Our brains are hardwired to focus on the negative. This is called **negative bias**, and it causes us to put more energy towards the negatives we find in ourselves instead of the positives.[3] This a protection mechanism that has allowed humans to survive for centuries.

4 Triggers for Low Self-Esteem

Self-esteem can fluctuate in different areas of our life. One day you're feeling great in a specific area, and the next day, the little voice in the back of your head is tearing you down again. Let's talk about the most common triggers for low self-esteem I've found in my 20 years of experience.

1. **Jealousy and self-comparison** always have the potential to make us second-guess our worth. When we start looking at our neighbors and comparing their success with our own, our self-esteem becomes triggered.

2. **Staying in toxic relationships** where we aren't valued is a massive knock to your self-esteem. If you surround yourself with toxic people who don't see your value, it will be harder for you to see your own self-worth. If you want

to heal from something, you have to separate yourself from the thing that makes you feel bad.

3. **Fear of not being enough.** Having a fear of not being smart enough, pretty enough, fit enough, or enough, in general, can trigger lasting feelings of low self-esteem.

4. **Holding on to past hurts.** When we hold on to anger and resentment from wounds in our past, it prevents us from fully loving life and being our best selves. If you're stewing in the pain of the past, you'll also find yourself struggling with self-esteem.

When you recognize something, you can change it. So, ask yourself which of the four self-esteem triggers (jealousy, toxic relationships, fear, or past hurts) you relate to most. Getting honest and comfortable with your triggers puts you on the right track to doing something about it.

4 Tools for Healthy Self-Esteem

Self-esteem is a skill you can build with practice. The more you recognize your triggers, the easier it is to shift the narrative and bring yourself back into the healthy zone of self-esteem. There are several steps you can take to work towards moving your self-esteem into the healthy zone.

1. **Be self-aware.** Self-awareness is the ability to see yourself clearly and objectively through reflection and introspection. Ask yourself a powerful question. Ask, "How am I feeling at this moment?" Practice being self-aware every day, and you will hone this skill.

2. **Take a non-judgmental perspective** on the thought you're having. Stop giving your thoughts so much power. Your thoughts do not define you. If you're feeling jealous, insecure, or scared, take a look at the thoughts and know that thought isn't necessarily true. This will stop you from spiraling into a cycle of shame.

3. **Replace negative thoughts** with neutral thoughts. Neutral thinking emphasizes judgment-free thinking, especially in crises and pressure situations. It's a realistic perspective on the situation that leaves room for all possibilities. Neutral thinking allows you to be honest about what you feel but leaves room for you to move forward.

   - **Example Negative Thought**: I failed my math test. I'm horrible at math and will probably fail this class.

   - **Example Neutral Thought:** I definitely bombed that math test, but I've done fairly well on other math tests, so I'll keep trying.

4. **Be intentional about remembering your wins.** Remember all the things you have accomplished, and that makes you proud. Give yourself evidence to support your value and worth.

When you find yourself struggling with self-esteem (as we all do sometimes), I want you to come back to this chapter, so you can identify your triggers and use the tools for healthy self-esteem. Everything takes time and practice, but with consistency, you can knock the self-esteem monster out of your life.

3.2 – Discussion Questions

1. Which of the 4 Triggers of Low Self-Esteem has the biggest effect on you, and why?

2. What is one negative thought you've had about yourself in the past? What are some ways you can replace that negative thought with a neutral thought?

3. Which of the 4 Tools for Healthy Self-Esteem do you need to work on the most in your life, and why?

4. If a friend told you that he or she was struggling with self-esteem, what are some positives ways you could help them?

3.3 – You've Always Been Good Enough

 Hey everyone, it's Dr. Kirleen, here with more insights on self-esteem. We've all experienced the feeling of being "not enough" …not being smart enough, pretty enough, tall enough, or good enough in some way. Feeling like you're not enough is as common as the sky is blue. As a therapist, I've helped doctors, lawyers, politicians, engineers, and other really smart people get out of their head and disrupt the "not enough" feeling.

And I'm not immune – as a teenager, I was the poster child for feeling not good enough. From hating my kinky, curly hair to thinking I had the worst acne to feeling like everyone else was smarter, I constantly questioned my value and worth. I didn't know as a teen that most of my peers were struggling with the same types of feelings.

In this section, I'm excited to share with you three key lessons for overcoming the "never good enough" feeling.

I'm not promising that feeling will go away forever, but I can tell you it can and will get a whole lot better as you work on it over time.

Lesson #1 – Don't Buy the Lie

If you believe you're "not enough" just the way you are, you will constantly try to fill the hole or compensate for the false sense of inadequacy. The thought that you are inadequate can feel so real, but your emotions are a poor indicator of what is real or not. This is because emotions are actually "outcomes" of what we think or perceive of a situation rather than something that determines how we think.

Psychologists have identified a behavior that explains why we buy the lie of not being enough. The term is called **emotional reasoning**. In short, emotional reasoning is the act of thinking something must be true simply because it "feels" true.[4] When you engage in emotional reasoning, you are tricked by weak logic, or you accidentally ignore any evidence contrary to your perspective. For instance, if you believe you're not smart enough, despite the fact you pass all your classes with A's and B's and have been told by teachers and parents how smart you are, then your inaccurate belief is based on emotional reasoning.

Lesson #2 – Control the Inner Critic

We all have one — an inner voice that expresses disapproval, criticism, or frustration about ourselves. It might sound like, "You're stupid," "You're a failure," "What's wrong with you?" or "Why can't you get it together?" Many of us don't even realize its presence because the critic's voice is different for each of us. The bottom line is that the inner critic sabotages your self-worth.

Awareness is the first step to controlling the inner critic. Catch yourself the next time you say something negative, critical, or ugly about yourself or about someone else. Identify how the situation triggered your inner critic. Ask yourself, "What are my honest feelings about this situation?" Allow yourself space to dig deep and find your most authentic feelings about what happened, how you feel, and why you feel that way.

Your next step is to dispute the critic. You can do this by pulling from evidence in your life that tells a different story. For example, if your inner critic says, "No one likes you," you can remind yourself that you have family, friends, teachers, or coaches who think you're great and enjoy spending time with you.

Lesson #3 – Do it Anyway

You get one life to do the things that light you up. Don't let the "not good enough" feeling get in your way. Even if you're scared or unsure of how things will work out, I want you to go for your dreams and never look back. This means you should try out for the team, ask the girl out, apply for the college of your dreams, or anything else that lights you up. Just do it! I'm not saying everything will work out correctly, but what I can tell you is that in the long run, you won't regret trying.

Anxiety & Overthinking

We've all been lost in thought at some point, but overthinking can go farther than that. Overthinking happens when one anxious thought or fear turns into another, and then another... until you've fallen down a rabbit hole in your mind. Sometimes, overthinking can lead to physical symptoms of anxiety, like increased heart rate, increased stress, and rising body temperature.[5]

If you find yourself overthinking or worrying about something, and you notice your thoughts spiraling out of control, you can break the cycle. To conquer your anxiety, you have to slow down the tendency to overthink simple situations. Practice mindfulness by bringing your attention back to the present moment. If you're in class, bring your attention back to your body at the desk, the sound of the classroom, or your work. If you're in the car, bring your attention back to the view out the windshield, the feeling of the AC, or the sound of the radio. If you're at home, go outside or find a quiet place indoors to just breathe and be fully present in the moment.

You Are Good Enough

Remember: you're not alone. Everyone (including the people you least expect) will occasionally get stuck overthinking or feeling like they're not good enough. If you use the lessons we shared in this chapter, you can learn how to shut down the lie of perfection and the voice of the inner critic. You can do this by getting comfortable being uncomfortable and facing your fears head-on. Also, don't forget that seeking help from a licensed mental health professional can help you shift any negative beliefs and direct your thoughts to a healthier sense of self-esteem.

3.3 – Discussion Questions

1. In Lesson # 1, Dr. Kirleen described the process of emotional reasoning. How can emotional reasoning affect the way we see a situation?

2. In what areas of your life have you ever felt not good enough? Is that voice coming from your inner critic or from some other person in your life?

3. When you're feeling anxious or overthinking everything, which of the three lessons (don't buy the lie, control the inner critic, and do it anyway) seems like a good first step for you, and why?

4. If you're struggling with self-esteem issues, remember you can always talk with a trusted adult, such as a parent, guardian, or mental health professional. You're not broken, you're merely a work in progress, just like everyone else.

Chapter 3 References

[1] Ackerman, C. (2020, October 31). What is Self-Esteem? A Psychologist Explains [2020 Update]. Retrieved November, 2020, from https://positivepsychology.com/self-esteem/

[2] Self-Esteem. Psychology Today. November, 2020, from https://www.psychologytoday.com/us/basics/self-esteem.

[3] Cherry, K. (2019, September 30). What is the Negative Bias? Verywell Mind. October 07, 2020 from https://www.verywellmind.com/negative-bias-4589618.

[4] Berle, D., & Moulds, M. L. (2013). Emotional reasoning processes and dysphoric mood: cross-sectional and prospective relationships. PloS one, 8(6), e67359. https://doi.org/10.1371/journal.pone.0067359

[5] National Institute of Mental Health, U.S. Department of Health and Human Services, (2016) "Generalized Anxiety Disorder: When Worry Gets Out of Control." www.nimh.nih.gov/health/publications/generalized-anxiety-disorder-gad/index.shtml.

Chapter 4

MENTAL ILLNESS & INJURY

4.1 –What is Mental Illness?

 Hey, y'all! Dr. OH here to talk about mental illness and how it can affect you in your teenage years. You've just learned about mental health, so what happens when we are mentally unhealthy? Let's get this out of the way first: **everyone** experiences temporary periods of being mentally unwell, just as everyone experiences periods of being physically unwell. In life, we sometimes get physically injured or hurt or even sick, and the same thing is true for our mind and our emotions. It's nothing to be ashamed of. It's part of being human.

If you think about the boat metaphor, every boat has to deal with waves and storms. Every boat has to keep an eye out for any leaks. Every boat needs to refuel, and so on. It would be absurd to think that your boat (your life) will have perfect weather (circumstances) 100% of the time. And of course, every boat needs maintenance from time to time – it's a normal part of being a boat.

Your mind needs maintenance, too!

Have you ever been super nervous about an upcoming event, like a class presentation or going on a date? You can't stop worrying about it. You might even lose sleep over it. Maybe your appetite changes or you feel sick to your stomach. Or maybe you have trouble concentrating on your daily tasks. Well, those are all symptoms of **anxiety** – something we'll talk about a lot in this book.

Have you ever been really sad or down in the dumps, like after a bad breakup, or maybe after the death of a loved one? You might lose interest in the things you usually love doing. Maybe you stop talking to people and you close yourself off in your room. You might have changes in your appetite and in your sleep patterns.

Well, those are all symptoms of **depression** – another topic we'll discuss at length in this book.

And of course, you eventually do the class presentation and you eventually go on that date, and the anxiety passes. And yes, the pain of losing an important relationship eventually fades (I promise), and the depression lifts. But in the meantime – when you're suffering, and when your boat has no fuel to get out of the storm – you're not mentally healthy. And it's okay to acknowledge that.

Does that mean you have a mental illness? No. Occasional trouble with mental health does not mean you have a **diagnosable mental disorder.**

When does being mentally unwell become a disorder?

How do you know when you're going through something more serious than one of life's usual mental speed bumps? You can't make a diagnosis on your own, but if all of the following points apply to you, it's time to talk to a mental health professional:

- You have multiple symptoms, **and…**

- The symptoms are so bad that they seriously interfere with your ability to live your daily life, **and…**

- The interference lasts for an extended period of time, such as several weeks or even months.

Those are the main three factors that set mental disorders apart from those mental speed bumps we were talking about. The most qualified source on mental illnesses is called the **Diagnostic and Statistical Manual of Mental Disorders, 5th edition.**[1] This manual is put together and used by experts to diagnose and treat mental illness. The vast majority of mental health workers consider it the definitive source for their profession.

KEEP IN MIND: The DSM-5 is written by mental health professionals… for mental health professionals. The wording is very academic, and it can be easy to misunderstand or oversimplify. The DSM-5 should never be formally or professionally used by anyone other than a trained and certified expert, like a doctor or a psychologist.

What is a Mental Health Professional?

Mental health professionals are people who have advanced college degrees in the field of mental health and are licensed to practice mental health in the state where they live. They have to complete many hours of training and pass difficult exams administered by their state become they can become a certified professional. Below is a brief look at the different types of mental health professionals:

- **Psychiatrists** have medical degrees (M.D.) and specialize in treating mental disorders using medication. A few psychiatrists will meet people for counseling or therapy sessions, but generally speaking they will refer you to another professional for that portion of your treatment.

- **Psychologists** have doctoral degrees (Ph.D., Psy.D.). They are also licensed by the state in which they practice. With very few exceptions, they do not prescribe medications. Instead, they have extensive training in recognizing mental illnesses and using different types of psychotherapy to treat them.

- **Counselors** and **Therapists** have master's degrees (M.S., M.A.) and specialize in a field of mental health. They have different licenses depending on their specialty and where they practice.

What about the family doctor – can they help? Primary care doctors have medical degrees but they are not mental health professionals. They are a good starting point for evaluating your symptoms and referring you to the types of professionals above. Because they are medical doctors, they can prescribe medication for mental illnesses but they are not trained to provide comprehensive mental health care.

You can find a full list of different mental health experts (and a ton of other great information) on the National Alliance on Mental Illness website at https://www.nami.org/.[2] Knowledge is power!

4.1 – Discussion Questions

1. What are some of the differences between being mentally unwell and having a mental illness or disorder?

2. If you suspect that you have a mental illness, can you diagnose yourself? Why not? How can you get help if you're struggling with mental health?

4.2 – What is Counseling or Therapy?

Hey everyone! It's Tom again, here to talk about the importance of counseling and therapy. Throughout this book whenever we talk about **counseling**, or **therapy**, or **talk therapy**, or **psychotherapy**, or **Cognitive Behavioral Therapy**, we mean basically the same thing: **meeting with a mental health professional to talk about your life, your mental health, and any challenges you're facing.** Being proactive about your mental health is a very positive thing!

The goal of counseling is to become aware of any self-defeating thought patterns or behaviors, so you can think more clearly and behave more effectively in the future.[3] There are many more types of counseling and therapy, but to keep things simple, we're referring to them all together in one big group.

Do you want to change something about yourself? Maybe you have an anger problem and you don't know where it's coming from. You wonder to yourself: *Why am I always yelling?*

Maybe you've been feeling depressed for a long time, and you wonder why your energy is so low. Or your anxiety in social situations is so strong, it's practically crippling.

Maybe something happened in your past, something horrible, and whenever the memory is triggered, your brain takes you right back to that moment.

Perhaps you have a secret addiction, and you're tired of being owned. Or maybe you're exhausted from trying to maintain a perfect image on social media.

Maybe you're just mad at your dad… or at your mom.

Maybe you've been stuffing your feelings down so deep that you feel numb to the world. Maybe the voice of **"you're never good enough"** is making you feel unlovable.

Whatever "**that thing**" is for you… clearly you don't like that about yourself. It's annoying, it's self-defeating, and you want to make a change, so you do the right thing: you go to counseling.

I went to counseling many times as a teen because I needed to get stuff out of my head. I struggled with depression, anxiety, self-esteem issues, behavioral problems, and family issues with my dad. I knew some of my thoughts and feelings were dragging me down, but until I went to counseling, I never knew how to make a change.

Today, I still go to counseling several times a year. Sometimes I go because I want help with a specific issue… similar to seeing a doctor when you're sick. Sometimes I go because I'm being proactive about my mental health… like working out at the gym. The cool thing is: counseling can be either location, the doctor's office or the gym, depending on what you need at the time.

Going to counseling or therapy should be seen as a normal part of life. These people are trained mental health professionals! They help you process your thoughts and feelings, so you can develop a better plan for your mental health and for your behavior.

How Counseling Sessions Work

Some counseling sessions are one-on-one (just you and the counselor), and some sessions take place in group settings, which is called group therapy. It really just depends on what you need and what you're trying to get out of it. Therapy sessions generally go around 50 minutes, give or take. I always feel like the time goes by very quickly… and I think that's because my soul needs to speak. It's a basic human need.

And bonus: therapy and counseling sessions are considered *confidential*, which is great because it means your therapist won't share your secrets with the world. That means you can open up and be honest about your actual thoughts and feelings. You can be your full, unapologetic self, and double-bonus: your counselor won't judge you.[4]

While therapists and counselors live by a code of confidentiality, they are also required by law to report severe incidents of abuse and neglect. This is called **"mandatory reporting."** If someone seriously hurt you or broke the law, counselors and therapists are considered "**mandatory reporters**," and they are required to report the incident to law enforcement or to child protective services. But that shouldn't scare you from talking to them. It's important to be totally honest with your counselor, so you can get the help you need. Mandatory reporting laws are really just there to protect you and the people around you.[5]

Counseling is Basic Self-Care

Let me be real with you: I love counseling. It's a very direct way to take care of yourself. I mean, where else can you go talk about your problems for an hour without feeling like you're hogging the conversation and making everything all about you? With counseling, *it's supposed to be all about you*, so you don't need to feel selfish for talking about your life. The therapist has one goal: *to help you discover... how to help yourself.*

If you need to talk with someone today, your school counselor is a good place to start. Or if you want to speak with someone outside of school, your parents or guardians can help you find a counselor or therapist who is a good fit for you. **The reality is:** you might not "click" right away with the first counselor, or even the second or third counselor, and that's okay.

Be honest with the adults in your life, so they can help you find the right person. The more comfortable you are with your counselor, the more you can open up and be real.

I know from experience: that's where you can find the leak in your boat. That's where you maintain your engine. And it's where you learn how to refuel, so you can start going places again.

If you ever feel like counseling might be a good idea, talk with your parents or guardians about it, and see if they can schedule an appointment for you with a mental health professional.

4.2 – Discussion Questions

1. **Let me give you a challenge.** I want you to think deeply about your life. Give yourself some time to think, so you can be honest, and ask yourself these questions: What thoughts are dragging me down? What behaviors do I want to change? Am I going through any "storms" in my life right now? If I could fix one "leak" in my boat, what would it be?

2. Even more importantly, I want you to ask: Who are the trusted adults in my life? Who are my positive influences and my "lighthouses" in the storm?

3. **Here's another challenge.** I want you to mentally step out of your own shoes for a minute. Try and fast-forward in your mind to five years from now, and look back at the person you are today. Does the teenager you're thinking about (meaning you) need to talk with someone?

4. If the answer is yes, then I'm asking you to please setup that appointment today. Set a reminder on your phone. Heck, write it on your hand if you have to. Just make sure to follow through. You're doing the right thing.

5. Take a few minutes to write a specific plan of action.

4.3 – Mental Illness and the Brain

Hey y'all, it's Dr. OH again. Let's imagine you accidentally hit your leg against the corner of a table. (Ouch!) It hurts for a few moments, but then the pain goes away. No biggie.

The next day you have a gnarly bruise where you hit your leg, and it's painful to the touch. (Ouch, again!)

Let me ask: ***does your leg hurt to touch because you hit it?*** You're probably thinking...*uh, duh!*

But in fact, hitting your leg yesterday is not the *direct* cause of your pain today. Hitting your leg broke blood vessels under the skin and the skin became inflamed. This inflammation – the bruise – now causes the pain. If you had hit your leg and not developed a bruise, things probably wouldn't be painful.

What does all of this have to do with mental health and your brain? A lot! Sometimes our life circumstances can lead to feelings of anxiety or depression, but the ***direct cause*** of those mental issues is an imbalance in brain chemistry. You don't get anxious because of an upcoming exam. You get anxious because of the way your brain chemistry deals with your knowledge of the exam.

Your brain chemistry is uniquely yours. It is the result of some combination of your genetics and your life experiences. No two brains work exactly the same way (which is why one person might get anxious about an upcoming event, while another person isn't bothered by it).

All of this basically means that you have more control over your life than you probably think. If you change the way your brain processes information, you can change the way you react to the world. The good news here is that your brain chemistry is super flexible. It responds to behavioral changes, cognitive changes (changing the way you think), medication, biofeedback (more on that when we talk about stress), and much more.

Because your brain is a one-of-a-kind 1st edition, the techniques and therapies that are best for someone else won't necessarily be the best for you. You have to work to find what works for you. Speaking with a mental health professional is a great way to discover what works for you, but you can also start by doing your own research. Here are some websites we recommend as great resources – check 'em out: the <u>American Psychological Association</u>, the <u>American Psychiatric Association</u>, and the <u>National Alliance on Mental Illness</u>.

Mental Health Shouldn't be Weird

As you grow up there are tons of physical changes going on in your body, and that definitely includes your brain. The brain you have as a teenager is not the brain you'll end up with as an adult. In fact, your brain doesn't really start leveling off development-wise until sometime in your twenties.

That means that mentally speaking, the playing field is constantly changing. And it means being a teen can sometimes be difficult, messy, emotional, and a host of other exhausting adjectives. That's why it's not weird to talk about mental health – to learn about it and take care of it. Because every teen is grappling with it. Check out these statistics on how many teens are affected by a diagnosed mental illness. The data below is from a 2019 study conducted by the U.S. Department of Health and Human Services.[6]

- Over 30% of teens (13-18 years old) have a diagnosed anxiety disorder. That only includes diagnosed cases. And that doesn't include the non-clinical anxiety that many teens experience on occasion.

- About 13% of teens (12-17 years old) have a diagnosed depressive disorder.

- About 9% of teens (13-18 years old) have diagnosed Attention Deficit Hyperactivity Disorder (ADHD).

And that's just scratching the surface. The numbers are way bigger if you consider teens who suffer from *mild anxiety* or *mild depression*. Of course, these are not diagnosable disorders – they are part of being human, and most people experience them from time to time in their lives (just as most people get bruises from time to time).

Thankfully, you now know that there are people who want to help you take charge of your mental health. With their help and your hard work, you can give your brain the resources it needs to be the best brain it can be. You won't regret it!

4.3 – Discussion Questions

1. Imagine yourself in the situations below. How anxious or nervous do these situations make you feel? Rate them on a scale of 1 to 5, with 5 being super nervous and 1 being not nervous at all.

a. You are about to jump out of a plane (with a parachute; you're not Iron Man).

b. You are about to ask someone you really like to have lunch with you.

c. You have a major test tomorrow.

d. You have to tell a friend terrible news.

e. The principal wants to talk to you immediately.

f. You just failed a test.

g. You come across a snake while talking a walk.

h. You're about to get your blood drawn at the hospital.

i. You are sitting in the park and a police officer approaches you.

j. You just walked on stage to perform in front of a lot of people.

2. Now, compare your answers to someone else's. Are they all the same? Some of them might be, because some situations cause a lot of brains to react the same way for survival purposes.

3. For example, many people will feel some amount of anxiety about jumping out of a plane or being near a snake. But some of your ratings won't be the same because of everyone's unique brain chemistry.

Chapter 4 References

[1] American Psychiatric Association. (2013). *Diagnostic and Statistical Manual of Mental Disorders: DSM-5*. https://www.psychiatry.org/psychiatrists/practice/dsm

[2] National Alliance on Mental Illness. (2020). *Types of Mental Health Professionals*. Retrieved August 8, 2020 from: https://www.nami.org/About-Mental-Illness/Treatments/Types-of-Mental-Health-Professionals.

[3] Mayo Clinic. (2019, March 16). Cognitive Behavioral Therapy. https://www.mayoclinic.org/tests-procedures/cognitive-behavioral-therapy/about/pac-20384610

[4] American Psychological Association. (2020). *Protecting Your Privacy: Understanding Confidentiality*. https://www.apa.org/topics/ethics-confidentiality

[5] Psychology Info. (2020, March 14). *Mandated Reporting*. https://psychology-info.com/mandated-reporting

[6] Department of Health and Human Services. (2019). *Common Mental Health Disorders in Adolescence*. Retrieved August 8, 2020 from: https://www.hhs.gov/ash/oah/adolescent-development/mental-health/adolescent-mental-health-basics/common-disorders/index.html

Chapter 5

COPING WITH GRIEF & LOSS

5.1 – Learning to Cope with Grief and Loss

Hey everybody, it's Tom again. Back when COVID-19 first made headlines, people who paid attention to the news had a few weeks to mentally adjust **before** all the lockdowns and quarantine went into effect. Even with all that advance notice, the pandemic immediately changed the daily routine for me, my wife, and our four kids. There was no certainty for my career. I usually speak at about 100 schools per year, but back in 2020, everything changed. On March 10th, I was speaking to six middle schools at a conference in New York, and then the very next day all of those schools went to full-time online classes. I flew back home and learned that all the rest of my upcoming school assemblies were cancelled… even for the following school year. I started to think about how the pandemic would affect the rest of the world, especially teens, and that's when I decided to write this book. Thankfully, I was able to recruit three amazing co-authors with different life experiences to help round out our perspectives.

One thing we all agree on is this: the pandemic was a life-changing, traumatic event, the kind that can lead to all kinds of mental health crises and challenges. Personally, I knew people who died from the corona virus, and that has been devastating, especially for their family members. But death isn't the only type of loss. There are endless types of pain and loss you may have experienced, and whenever you experience loss, you need tools to make the best of a difficult situation.

What about you? How have you experienced grief or loss in your own life. One of the common mistakes we make as adults is telling young people to *just think positive, get over it, and move on.* But that's usually not the best solution because it doesn't give our minds enough time to process what happened and to express grief for the loss we experienced.

The Stages of Grief

Psychiatrist Elisabeth Kübler-Ross first came up with the idea of "The Stages of Grief" as way to deal with death and loss. Back in the 1970s and 80s, Kübler-Ross identified **five stages of grief**.[1] Then in 2019, David Kessler, a grief expert who had worked with Kübler-Ross, added a **sixth stage: finding meaning**.[2] Let's use divorce as an example of loss. Here's what the stages might look like:

1. **Denial:** My parents are not getting a divorce. It's impossible.

2. **Anger:** I hate that my parents are getting a divorce.

3. **Bargaining:** If I really behave myself, maybe they'll get back together.

4. **Depression:** No one cares anyway. It's pointless.

5. **Acceptance:** The divorce happened, but I'm able to move forward.

6. **Meaning:** The divorce hurt, but it also helped me become more resilient.

Identifying the stages when you experience a loss can help you realize that what you're feeling is normal and expected. If a friend or a family member died, for example, you might feel more anger than sadness – but knowing about the stages of grief helps you accept your feelings as part of the process.

It's important to note: we usually do not move through the stages of grief in a straight line. You might feel **anger at first, then denial, then anger and denial at the same time.** You might become **depressed before feeling angry**. The stages of grief help you understand the different feelings you'll likely experience during a loss, not the order in which to feel them.

When you experience a significant loss, it can take a very long time to feel normal again. There are steps you can take to help yourself feel better, but it always takes time. You need time to accept the loss, experiencing your grief and pain, adjust to your new reality, and ultimately continue on with your life.[3] Sometimes your mind might accept a loss, but your emotions take longer to catch up. You might know and accept that your uncle passed away, but you still cry every time you think about him. That's ok. It's a normal part of the grieving process.[4]

Finding Support

When you're grieving, lots of people want to support you, but sometimes it can be hard to accept their support. You might feel like no one knows what you're really going through. And of course, it's frustrating to hear friends or family brush it off saying things like "it will be ok" or "everything happens for a reason." Still, connecting with people in your support system is important for your healing. Try to let them know your true feelings without pushing them away. Instead of snapping when they tell you that "it's for the best," ask them instead to share memories of your loved one, or have them tell about a time they were grieving. This can make you feel less alone, and it might even bring you closer together.

If your friend is grieving, focus on being there for her. She might want to talk about what happened, or she might not want to talk. It's possible she will want to make small talk about school or the weather, and all of this is okay. Listen to her needs, and be there for her. Sometimes, distraction is good for people who are grieving, and other times they want to talk about deep topics like what happens when we die. Meet your friends and family where they're at – it's even okay to ask them how you can best support them during their grief.

5.1 – Discussion Questions

1. What were some of the losses you've experienced in your life?

2. Which loss was the most significant to you, and how are you handling it?

3. Can you see yourself somewhere in the stages of grief? How so?

4. Has anyone ever encouraged you to just get over it and move on? If so, how did that make you feel? Is moving on always the best solution?

5. How can understanding the stages of grief help you support a friend or family member when they experience a loss?

5.2 – Coping with Difficult Seasons of Life

Hey y'all, it's Dr. OH again. As Tom said, the pandemic completely changed life as we know it. It slammed into our metaphorical boats with some serious hurricane force. Our daily routines have screeched to a halt. We can't even hang out with friends and family. School and work are a whole new ballgame. So, I want to ask you – how are you? How have you been handling this mess?

Maybe you're feeling worried, bored, annoyed, sad, overwhelmed, or all of the above. These feelings are normal and valid, and your experience of them is unique. A lot of people are having an equally difficult time with their feelings right now. Even us old folk (aka adults) are struggling with all of the changes surrounding the pandemic. In times of uncertainty, anyone and everyone's mental health can take a hit. It's just hard to know how to feel, what to think, and the right thing to do in a situation that no living person has ever been through.

Below are five ways to stay mentally healthy during difficult times.[5]

1. Research The Cause of Your Anxiety. Things we don't understand can be scary, so always do your research. Don't just find the research you want to find to confirm your opinions – find the facts. Find sources with good reputations. Find information that is current and confirmed by multiple sources (if possible). Don't get sucked into rumors and fear mongering. If you do your best to find the facts, you'll have more control over your situation.

2. Schedule time to be social. With social distancing practices everywhere, it's easy to feel lonely. It's really important that you get the friend and family time that you need. Making time to connect and stay in touch with those you love can lift your mood and help keep your mental health in check. You can text, call, and use services like FaceTime, WhatsApp and other video conferencing apps. Just be smart about social media like Facebook, Instagram, Snapchat, and the like. Don't let yourself be dragged down by negativity, and don't forget that other people are also struggling right now.

3. Take Time to Relax. Relaxing is an essential component of self-care and it's a great way to re-fuel your boat. The terms "relaxation" and "self-care" mean something different to everyone. For some, a long bath with a good book does the trick. Some create art, others enjoy it. For still others, different kinds of exercise or sports can help them destress. Anything you can (safely) do to give your mind a break will go a long way toward maintaining your mental health overall. #TreatYoSelf

4. Talk about your feelings. This can go hand in hand with being social. You should be regularly sharing your feelings with a person(s) you trust. It's normal to have a mishmash of emotions right now – it's hard enough to be in a pandemic, let alone be a teenager in a pandemic! Talking with someone can help you feel connected and remind you that you're not alone, so don't be afraid to open up about your personal experience. Friends, family, church, and teammates are all good examples of places to find the support you need.

5. Ask for help. Having the self-awareness to know when you need assistance is an admirable trait. If you feel like your mental health is suffering, the best course of action is to talk with a trained mental professional like a doctor, licensed counselor, psychologist, or psychiatrist. Most of them take online appointments, so you don't even have to mask-up.

Remember: No human being currently alive has been through anything like this. **We're all experiencing it for the first time together.** Making mental health a priority helps us work together and remain calm in the storm.

5.2 – Discussion Questions

1. What kinds of things cause you the greatest stress or anxiety?
2. What are some healthy activities you can do to manage stress or anxiety?
3. When you're feeling alone or isolated, what are some things you can do to feel connected and heard?

5.3 –How to Navigate Difficult Conversations

Hey Guys! It's Dr. Kirleen again! I'm here to tackle the issue of difficult conversations. In today's world, we are being faced with difficult topics more than ever. I personally have been having difficult conversations with clients, friends, and neighbors who want to know my stance on the Black Lives Matter movement as an African American woman. These conversations can be intimidating, and divisive. The good news is: I've found that having these uncomfortable conversations has opened up the door for a deeper level of connection with my friends because we are no longer pretending that race and politics don't matter. They do matter, and we can learn a lot from listening and trying to understand each other.[6]

Why People Avoid Difficult Conversations

Having difficult conversations is a part of life. Speaking openly and honestly about our thoughts and feelings helps us navigate relationships, negotiate job offers, and speak the truth on important topics. But many times, these conversations never take place because people simply avoid having them in the first place. Why do we do that? Let's look to psychology for some answers.

Anxiety Around the Conversation Going Poorly: Many people avoid having difficult conversations because they're afraid it will go wrong. You start visualizing the other person getting offended, emotional, and walking away. Before you know it, you've already experienced the worst-case scenario in your head. That's called "catastrophizing." If we think we're walking into a disaster, naturally we want to avoid it.

Fear of Rocking the Boat: It's hard to raise a concern when everything seems to be going smooth in a relationship. Sometimes we worry if we bring up a problem, then we will be seen as the problem. Imagine one of your friends said an offensive joke at school. Perhaps it was about women's rights, or LGBTQ issues, or racism in America. Clearly, what they said was hurtful, and you know you need to say something. (Honestly, it would be easier to speak up if this person wasn't your friend!) Sometimes people stay silent in a relationship for fear of "rocking the boat."

Fear of Losing the Relationship: Fear of losing a relationship is the core concern behind why people avoid difficult conversations. You worry that speaking your mind will cause others to withdraw from you and eventually end the relationship altogether. This is a valid fear, and that's why it's essential to know how to handle yourself. Remember: a difference of opinion doesn't have to end a friendship.

How to Prepare Ahead of Time

- Ask yourself what you want out of the conversation. Are you coming from a place of respect and curiosity, or are you trying to settle a score or make yourself feel better? Understand where you're coming from and what you're trying to achieve before anything else.

- Stop "catastrophizing" about it. If you're already envisioning a negative outcome in your head, then it can become a self-fulfilling prophecy… meaning you accidentally make it come true. You become hesitant and awkward, and you come across differently than you intended.

- Check your emotional state ahead of time. You don't want to enter a difficult conversation if you're feeling anxious, angry, or emotional. It's important to have a clear head. If you're flooded with emotion, things can get out of hand.

- Gather facts over fiction. If you're gearing up to have a conversation around human rights or anything political, make sure you have your facts straight. And that doesn't mean watching a YouTube video to prepare. You need to go to the sources of the facts and see them for yourself before presenting them to someone else.

7 Tools for Difficult Conversations

It's necessary to have difficult conversations because not speaking about problems rarely makes situations go away but often results in increased stress and unhappiness. Once you've completed all your prep work, you're ready to have the difficult conversation. Below are seven tools to help things run smoothly.

1. **Approach the conversation from a place of curiosity.** Bring your empathy and do your best to put yourself in the other person's shoes. When people realize you are genuinely curious, they are less likely to be defensive.

2. **Listen more than you talk.** Be receptive to what the other party has to say. Instead of thinking of your next response while they talk, absorb what they are saying. Be an active listener to make the conversation more productive.[7]

3. **Validate their position.** This is an important one because it lets the other party know they are being heard. Tell them you understand where they're coming from and how they've reached their conclusions.

4. **Use positive body language.** If your words and your body language are saying two different things, you can accidentally make the other party feel alienated or even attacked. Rolling your eyes or crossing your arms can come across as condescending. Here's a great article to learn the basics of body language: https://www.mindtools.com/pages/article/Body_Language.htm.

5. **Speak your truth.** You cannot have a difficult conversation without speaking your truth. Respectfully conveying your thoughts and opinions, while taking time to hear theirs is the whole point. If you walk away without stating your truth, it will feel like a waste of time.

6. **Maintain your composure.** You can only control yourself. You can't control the other person's reactions, and you can't control the full outcome of the conversation. By maintaining your self-control, you take the high road, even if they take the low road. (You can credit former First Lady, Michelle Obama, for this important insight.)

7. **Press pause when needed.** If the person you're speaking with is getting agitated or angry, don't take the bait. Try to steer the conversation back to empathy and respect. If it continues getting heated, you might need to agree to stop the conversation and return to it at a later time. If the other person has respect for you, they should be willing to do the same.

Even when you do your part and stay respectful, some conversations will still end poorly. That's also part of life. By using the seven tools above, you can make sure to communicate clearly and walk away with no regrets.

5.3 – Discussion Questions

1. What are some reasons that people tend to avoid difficult conversations?

2. Think about a difficult conversation you may need to have with a friend, your parents, or family member. What are some ways you can prepare for the conversation ahead of time?

3. What is a topic that you feel passionate about? Share your feelings about a that topic and describe how you would handle a conversation with someone who has an opposing view.

Chapter 5 References

[1] Grief.com. The Five Stage of Grief, July, 2020. Retrieved from https://grief.com/the-five-stages-of-grief/.

[2] Grief.com. Finding Meaning: The Sixth Stage of Grief by David Kessler. (2019, Nov. 5). Retrieved, 2020 from https://grief.com/sixth-stage-of-grief/.

[3] Kornfeld, J., Waters, S., & Furgang, K. (2013). Death and Bereavement. Rosen Pub.

[4] Stages of Grief. (2020, December). Retrieved from Wikipedia.com. https://en.wikipedia.org/wiki/Five_stages_of_grief.

[5] "Support for Teens and Young Adults." Centers for Disease Control and Prevention, Centers for Disease Control and Prevention. Retrieved from www.cdc.gov/coronavirus/2019-ncov/daily-life-coping/stress-coping/young-adults.html.

[6] Family Conflict: How to Navigate Political Conversations. (2020, August 05). November, 2020, from https://onlinecounselingprograms.com/blog/family-conflict-how-to-navigate-political-conversations/.

[7] Kunst, J. (2016). How to Make Political Conversations More Productive. December, 2020, from https://www.psychologytoday.com/us/blog/headshrinkers-guide-the-galaxy/201607/how-make-political-conversations-more-productive.

Chapter 6

BULLYING

6.1 – How to Stop Bullying and Cyberbullying

Hey everybody, it's Tom again. I experienced a lot of bullying back in my day. As a kid, I was the shortest guy, so they called me "big guy." I had allergies and asthma and an inhaler, so they called me "bubble boy." As a teen, people made fun of my voice, my intelligence, and even… what they said was my sexuality.

Sometimes I'd get super mad and storm off. Other times, I'd try to get even and say something mean back to them… and neither of those reactions worked in the long run. I didn't have a plan for how to respond, so I would just… REACT without thinking. Whenever I stormed off, they knew they had me, and whenever I fought back (with my words, of course), then I was just lowering myself to their level. There is a way to speak up for yourself and be a strong person but without stooping to their level (more on that later).

I was stuck in the bullying cycle, and the worst part was… even after the bullying was done, I continued to give these hurtful people power over my thoughts and attitudes. I got bitter and resentful, and I wanted them to get what they deserved.

I was accidentally giving the bullies all this negative head space! If my mind was like an apartment building, they had moved in, and I was giving them free rent!

I was giving them power, and that's exactly what bullying is all about. Bullying is a power-grab between people of the same social status (two students for example).

The National Definition of Bullying

Since 2012 I've spoken at over 800 schools and conferences on the topics of bullying and mental health, and I'm constantly reminded that kids and teens need to learn the difference between *bullying* and *teasing.* After all, that is the most common excuse for bullying… "I WAS JUST JOKING!" To me the difference is simple. **Teasing** is playful and it happens among friends. And you know they're a friend because if you asked them to stop, they would… stop. (Duh!)

For the definition of bullying, let's look at StopBullying.gov. That's right, the U.S. Government has a website where they provide the national definition of bullying, and here it is…

The StopBullying.gov Definition of Bullying

Bullying is unwanted, aggressive behavior among school aged children that involves a real or perceived power imbalance. The behavior is repeated, or has the potential to be repeated, over time. Both kids who are bullied and who bully others may have <u>serious, lasting problems</u>.

In order to be considered bullying, the behavior must be aggressive and include:

- **An Imbalance of Power:** Kids who bully use their power—such as physical strength, access to embarrassing information, or popularity—to control or harm others. Power imbalances can change over time and in different situations, even if they involve the same people.

- **Repetition:** Bullying behaviors happen more than once or have the potential to happen more than once.

Bullying includes actions such as making threats, spreading rumors, attacking someone physically or verbally, and excluding someone from a group on purpose.

Types of Bullying

- **Verbal bullying** is saying or writing mean things. Verbal bullying includes:
  - Teasing
  - Name-calling
  - Inappropriate sexual comments
  - Taunting
  - Threatening to cause harm

- **Social bullying**, sometimes referred to as relational bullying, involves hurting someone's reputation or relationships. Social bullying includes:
  - Leaving someone out on purpose
  - Telling other children not to be friends with someone
  - Spreading rumors about someone
  - Embarrassing someone in public

- **Physical bullying** involves hurting a person's body or possessions. Physical bullying includes:
  - Hitting/kicking/pinching
  - Spitting
  - Tripping/pushing
  - Taking or breaking someone's things
  - Making mean or rude hand gestures

I always include **Cyberbullying** as the 4th type of bullying, but people often debate whether or not cyberbullying should get its own category. Technically speaking, *cyberbullying can be defined as* any type of <u>verbal</u> or <u>social bullying</u> that takes place between digital devices (like phones, computers, or gaming systems).

Whether you think there are three types of bullying or four types is a little beside the point. Either way, **one main point should be very clear: bullying is about power… it's a power grab between peers** – meaning people who should be entitled to the same social situation: two kids, two teens, two adults, or two co-workers. Bullying can also happen in groups of three or more, for example, if a handful of students gang up on someone.

And then there's that confusing phrase in the national definition where it says bullying happens *"among school aged children."* If that's the case, then why do colleges hire me to speak about bullying and cyberbullying? Why do large corporations like Starbucks hire me to speak to their employees on the topic of bullying? (Which, they did!) The point is: bullying can happen among adults too!

As far as I can tell, the reason the national definition uses the phrase *"among school aged children"* is to clarify an important point. They were trying to point out the difference between **bullying** and an **abuse of power**. When a student is repeatedly mean to another student, that is **bullying**. However, when a teacher is repeatedly mean to a student, that is an **abuse of power**. Make sense? Teachers are in a position of authority over students, so they should never abuse their power. And most of them don't, by the way. Most teachers are great people!

Bullying happens when you keep picking on one of your peers in a way that is hurtful of controlling. But still, there are exceptions. People often ask me, *"Does it have to be repeated to be considered bullying?"* Well, the answer is no! Take another look at the national definition. Twice it mentions behaviors that *"have the potential to be repeated over time."* What does that mean, exactly? It means there are some things you could do, and even if you only did it **one time**, it would be considered bullying.

Next question: where is that line? (The line of one-time bullying.)

For *physical bullying*, the line of one-time bullying is pretty clear. If you're aggressively putting your hands on someone, even one time, you're either bullying them or something worse (if you punch someone in the face, for example, that is considered a physical assault, which is a crime, aka, even worse than bullying).

If there is ever a threat of physical violence, or if anyone could be in any kind of danger, you need to call 911 right away! Safety is always the top priority.

Showing Respect for Everyone (Even When We Disagree)

When we talk about the other three types of bullying: **verbal**, **social**, and **cyberbullying**, these incidents can be harder to define. It often starts out with teasing or being rude (someone makes fun of your clothes, for example). As a one-time incident, that would usually not be considered bullying. But if a person repeatedly teases you for your clothes, it can turn into bullying.

The line of one-time bullying can be summed up in a single word: **identity**. Each person's unique identity *(their skin color, body shape, gender, sexuality, and religion, for example)* is a very important and special part of them. A person's identity should never be part of public ridicule. Those topics are private, and they should be discussed in private conversations between students and the trusted adults in their lives (their parents, guardians, school counselors, or mental health professionals).

But what about hot topics like gender identity and sexuality? What I'm saying is this: gender identity and sexual orientation should never be used as a way of bullying or harassment. These are very personal and sensitive topics.

Do we all have to share the same options on these topics? Of course not! But we have to treat everyone with respect and dignity. Every single person is 100% valuable… even the people we disagree with.

By reading this section, you may think you know my personal opinions on these topics, but I am doing exactly what I recommend: I'm keeping my opinions to myself, and I'm showing 100% respect and dignity to everyone.

If you want to talk about LGBTQ+ issues or about your gender or sexuality, I recommend talking to the people I mentioned above: your parents, guardians, school counselors, and adult mentors.

How to Speak Up Against Bullying

1. The first step is to **GET HELP FROM A TRUSTED ADULT** (such as your parents or guardians). I got help from my English Teacher, Mrs. Burdick. She listened to me and helped me see the big picture. Eventually I got counseling which helped even more!

2. I learned how to **STOP REACTING** (which means acting before thinking). Whenever I gave a knee-jerk response, I was giving the bullies exactly what they wanted – a reaction! I was giving them power.

3. I learned how to **START RESPONDING** (which means thinking through your actions ahead of time). I decided I wasn't going to cry about it, but I also wasn't going to bully them back. My counseling sessions helped me realize my greatest power was using my voice to firmly speak up against bullying. I said things like, "Knock it off!" and "You can't say stuff like that..." and "Wow, I guess you like to raise yourself up by putting other people down." And sometimes I decided to simply walk away, so I didn't get too fired up or say something I would regret.

There is no one-size fits all solution to bullying or cyberbullying. That means you need to use the tools in your toolbox (the actions that fit with your personality) to speak up against bullying in a way that is both powerful and positive at the same time. For some people, it means speaking up in the moment. Other people can brush it off with a joke. Some people need to walk away. And of course, you can always help out afterward… by reporting the bullying incident to your parents and your school, by telling a friend when they crossed a line, or by checking on the kid who was bullied and making sure they get from a trusted adult.

6.1 – Discussion Questions

1. What do you think is the difference between **bullying** and **teasing?** When does teasing turn into bullying?

2. In this chapter, Tom described the line of "one-time bullying" – where an incident can be considered bullying even if it happens only once. What do you think he meant by that?

3. What are some examples of how to speak up against bullying and/or cyberbullying **in the moment?**

4. What are some examples of how to speak up against bullying and/or cyberbullying **after the moment has passed?**

5. Take some time to explore StopBullying.gov. Look at the specific anti-bullying laws for your state, and ask yourself (or your group), *how is my school doing at following the anti-bullying laws?*

6. What is your school's solution for reporting bullying and cyberbullying? If your school doesn't have a clear solution, we recommend going to NoBullyingSchools.com – a website founded by Tom Thelen – and looking at the Report Bullying Smartphone App.

6.2 – Creating a Culture of Respect & Civility

Hey guys! It's Dr. Kirleen, back again to talk about civility! You should already know the importance of being polite, considerate, and kind. The saying, "treat others the way you want to be treated," may sound a little old school, but it's more needed than ever before. Many Americans believe civility is on the decline, and you might agree. We've all heard stories about bullying, naming calling, and hate speech. These events are happening in homes, classrooms, on the internet, and in the streets. It seems that uncivil people have gotten a free pass to say whatever they want.

Why has our culture become less civil? Some theories suggest that as society becomes more informal, we no longer have agreed-upon rules for respectful behavior. People also blame the popularity of reality TV shows because most of these shows are filled with back-stabbing rude behavior. Social media platforms have also made it easy for haters to post vicious and nasty comments anonymously.

What is Civility?

Civility is defined as polite behavior that supports social harmony and respects the humanity of individuals. Civility is vital in maintaining a society. There are several aspects to civility, some of which you probably already practice. Having good manners, effective listening skills, and tolerance can go a long way with civility. Empathy and the ability to recognize your mistakes is also an essential piece of being civil.[1]

The Consequences of Incivility

The opposite of civility is incivility. Incivility means being intentionally rude or unsociable toward others. In other words, trash talk. Unfortunately, incivility is a common practice. Technology has emboldened bullies to say things online they would never say face-to-face.[2] The real consequence of incivility is an increase in bullying, violence, and hate-filled behavior Studies show that incivility leads to violence, political division, unhealthy communities, and conflict.[3]

The consequence of incivility hit home for me a few years ago. The son of one of my colleagues committed suicide after being brutally bullied on social media by a group of classmates. You never know what will push someone over the edge, so adults and responsible teens need to foster civility in our schools and communities.

Digital Civility

Ninety-three percent of Americans believe there is a civility issue in America, and most of them blame the rise of social media. Over the years, the number of uncivil interactions happening online has grown exponentially. This is because social media provides an outlet for people to voice their opinions without face-to-face repercussions. In other words, people are more likely to spread hate speech when they can hide behind a computer or a smartphone. Of course, people have the right to their opinion, but it's become a huge trend to express opinions in an uncivil way online.[4]

People do this because, as humans, we want to be right. We are very attached to our opinions, and proving ourselves correct can outweigh civility. On social media, things can turn ugly with a tap of a button, and once those posts are out there, you can never get them back. Even if you post something and decide to delete it five seconds later, someone may have already taken a screenshot and shared your post with the world.

The best way to handle incivility online is to ignore it. Don't play into other people's drama, and only express your opinion if you can do so in a respectful, civil manner. In other words, if you don't have anything nice to say, don't say anything at all. (That's the loving mom in me, letting you know I want what's best for you.)

Enhancing Civility

In a world of growing incivility, you can become a role model by demonstrating respect and courtesy for everyone, even when we disagree (especially when we disagree!). People usually throw civility out the window when they're angry, frustrated, or scared. Remember, you are in control of your thoughts and actions. Keep your cool, and no one can get to you!

Below are 4 tips for enhancing civility:

1. **Be courteous to everyone.** Being polite to others is more than saying "please" and "thank you," even though that is important. Show good manners when others are presenting their opinions to you. Don't say anything that you wouldn't want to hear from them.

2. **Have empathy for others.** You'll never understand where everyone is coming from all the time. Try to put yourself in their shoes before responding.

Consider where they are coming from and what challenges they may be facing.

3. **Show tolerance for differences.** Be tolerant of others, even if they are different from you. Celebrate the differences instead of shying away from them. You may gain a new perspective!

4. **Be a good listener.** Being a good listener is a huge part of being civil. Hear others out before judging or speaking on their opinions. Instead of thinking about your next response while they're speaking, be present in the moment. You may find that you have more in common than you thought.

6.2 – Discussion Questions

1. What is civility, and how can you demonstrate it at school?

2. Do you think civility is on the rise, why or why not?

3. Why do you think some people are less civil when using social media?

4. If you were to notice a friend being uncivil (or rude or mean) to a certain group of people, what could you do?

5. What are some specific actions you can take to be more respectful and accepting with people who may look or seem different than you?

Chapter 6 References

[1] 7 Ways to Teach Children Civility. November, 2020, from https://www.theedadvocate.org/7-ways-teach-children-civil.

[2] The Age of Incivility: The Loss of Civil Communication on Social Media. (2020, March 23). From https://www.starrgates.com/the-age-of-incivility-the-loss-of-civil-communication-on-social-media/.

[3] Mitchell 2015. Civility 101: Who's Teaching the Class? From https://www.rootsofaction.com/civility-101-whos-teaching-the-class/.

[4] Stein, L. (2019, August 27). Study: Most Americans believe social media is causing incivility. From https://www.campaignlive.com/article/study-americans-believe-social-media-causing-incivility/1589096.

Chapter 7

EMOTIONAL INTELLIGENCE

7.1 – How to Develop Emotional Intelligence

Hey y'all! Dr. OH here to talk about emotional intelligence. Before we get into the emotion stuff, let's talk a little bit about **intelligence**. When we think of intelligence one of the first words that usually comes to mind is "smart". And "smart" is usually thought of in terms of book-smart: if you get good grades, then you're smart, therefore you're intelligent. But there are lots of different kinds of intelligence. Some people are street-smart and know how to be successful in an urban (city) environment. Some people are nature-smart and know how to survive and thrive in nature. Then there are the socially smart people who understand social dynamics and how to get along with other folks. Of course, there are also artists, who have creative intelligence.

In fact, there are so many different ways to be intelligent that even the experts can't agree on a definition that really covers everything. The one thing they can agree on is that intelligence has multiple components – it is not just a single entity that you have or don't have. Over the years, psychologists have developed tests (so. many. tests.) to try to measure all of the core components of intelligence and come up with a number to represent them. The current, most widely used test is the Weschler Adult Intelligence Scale, 4th edition.[1] This test results in a number score that is called the Intelligence Quotient, or **IQ**. Your IQ is a measure of your intelligence score compared to the scores of others in your age group. Despite the acceptance of this IQ measurement, the WAIS-IV does not have any subtests aimed at gauging the emotional component of your intelligence.

How are Emotions Part of Intelligence?

Emotional intelligence (**EI**; sometimes referred to as EQ or emotional quotient) is about how well you understand, manage, and communicate your own emotions. It involves successfully using your emotions to help guide your actions and decisions. It also includes how well you are able to interpret the emotions of others. That means having the "ability to read nonverbal channels, tone of voice, gesture, facial expression and the like", according to Daniel Goleman who popularized the concept of EI.[2]

Being able to control your anger and how you behave when you're angry is a form of EI. Knowing when your friend is sad, even when they tell you they're fine is also your EI at work. So, where does EI come from? Well, you know I love brains, so here goes another brain story…

Emotional Intelligence and the Brain

The two main areas of the brain involved in EI are the **limbic system** and the **prefrontal cortex**. The limbic system is made up of a few different structures that are considered to be the brain's emotional centers. The prefrontal cortex (PFC) is the front part of your brain – right behind your eyes. This area is involved in things like impulse control, reasoning, judgement, and decision-making.

Your limbic system and PFC "talk" to each other in order to manage emotions. Your limbic system signals ANGER, and your prefrontal cortex figures out the best course of action for dealing with that emotion. Should I yell? Hit something? Take deep breaths? Go for a run?

Here's the tricky part: your PFC isn't fully developed until you're about 25 years old! Which means that until you're a young adult, your PFC isn't fully prepared to handle all of your emotional decision-making. But that doesn't mean you can say, "I'm not responsible for my decisions! My prefrontal cortex isn't fully developed!" The very act of reasoning, and decision-making is what helps your PFC develop the way that it does. When you take responsibility for those decisions, you learn from them. As you learn, your brain forges physical connections between your limbic system and PFC. These connections are made of neurons, the special cells in your brain that we talked about in the section on Brain Basics. The neurons send communications back and forth between the two brain areas. The better the connections, the better the communication, the better the emotional intelligence.

7.1 – Discussion Questions

1. How does emotional intelligence fit onto your boat? What part of the boat relates to your limbic system and emotions? What part of the boat relates to your prefrontal cortex and your ability to make decisions and use judgment?

2. Think of a recent situation where you used your emotional intelligence to make a decision. Was your decision successful? Why? If not, what did you learn from it and how will you use that experience the future?

7.2 – Why Emotional Intelligence Matters

Hello students, Dr. Kagan here. Have you ever heard phrases like these? **"Suck it up," "Don't be such a cry baby," or "Don't be a wuus!"** I heard messages like that throughout much of my childhood and youth from my well-intentioned parents, brothers, friends, and educators. What was that all about? The senders of those messages were echoing their own discomfort with emotions. They were basically telling me to bury or hide my emotions, or that expressing emotions was a sign of weakness. As a kid, I remember feeling bad about myself … thinking something was wrong with me that I could not dismiss or put aside my emotions. I struggled and disliked that aspect of myself and sometimes my very identity. Thank my lucky stars I eventually got help for this. Fast-forward to my adult life, working as a school psychologist at a middle school in New York. My goal has always been to help kids develop a healthier way of understanding and regulating their emotions. So, let's discuss how the skill of emotional intelligence unlocks the secret to liking and loving ourselves, our life, and the people and the world around us.

Simply put, our emotions matter! They are an essential part of us. Our daily lives are filled with emotion and they are incredibly powerful. They drive how we think, learn, the decisions we make, and our behavior.[3] Did you ever feel so excited waking up to find that school had been cancelled due to a snow day or bad weather? How great that felt. Or did you ever feel so nervous or anxious and flooded with anxiety when you realized you forgot you were having a test next period? Dread and despair overwhelm your very being. You are having emotions every moment of your life and by allowing yourself to have emotions, acknowledging them and valuing them, it will allow you to use them wisely.[4]

We should never feel "at-fault" for our feelings and emotions. In his book, *Emotional Intelligence*, author Daniel Goldman explains **"our mind does not decide what emotions we should have!"**[5] As a matter of fact, mental health specialists and researchers who study emotions always emphasize not to "live in denial" of your feelings but be aware of them. All types of feelings give us important information. Positive feelings (such as joy and happiness) and negative feelings (such as anger and disgust) are important to recognize within ourselves. According to Dr. Marc Brackett of the Yale Center for Emotional Intelligence, the key step is giving ourselves **_Permission to Feel_** all of our feelings. That is the title of Dr. Brackett's book on emotional intelligence (highly recommended).

Feelings are the very essence of being human. Through our understanding of our emotions and the emotions of those around us, and acting on our emotions in a healthy way, we can be our best selves. Emotions really do matter! They inspire us to do good in this world, to be successful and have fun, to prepare us for danger or for challenge, to motivate us and to connect with others.

If we press pause to look internally, we can become more mindful, and we can start to recognize and respond to our emotions. **Mindfulness** is the ability to observe your own thoughts and feelings without judging them as good or bad. Recognizing our emotions for what they are (and without denying them) is the first step in developing emotional intelligence.

7.2 – Discussion Questions

1. Close your eyes and imagine a typical school day. Think about the moment when you awake, what it feels like getting up in the morning. Think about getting ready for school and what that feels like. Think about the emotions that happen when you're getting ready to go out the door. Are you feeling rushed, anxious, or excited? Or perhaps are you feeling calm as you head out the door to school? What are you feeling?

2. Now think about the school day itself – going to class or remote learning. Maybe you forgot to complete an important assignment – how does that feel? How does it feel to have a tough conversation with a friend? How do you feel when someone posts something rude about you online? How do you feel when you make the team, win the part in the play, or get asked to the school dance? How do you feel when you are deciding where to sit during lunch? Think about all the feelings you have throughout the school day.

3. Think about the end of the school day and what it feels like to go home. What do you feel as you interact with your family? As you use your phone and social media? What do you feel toward the end of the night when you're getting ready for bed?

4. Throughout the day, what are some examples when you might experience some negative feelings? What are some examples of when you might have positive feelings?

5. How do your feelings impact your thoughts, attitudes, and your actions?

7.3 – A Map for our Emotions

 Hey, it's Dr. Kagan again. Once we're aware of our emotions and feelings, what do we do next? Let me give you the "road map" or the steps to good mental health and happiness. Dr. Marc Brackett, founding director of the Yale Center for Emotional Intelligence, is one of the world's leading experts on emotional intelligence. I've been to Yale University to attend his trainings in person and to learn about a wonderful tool called "RULER" which serves as a roadmap for our emotions. Let's look at what each letter in RULER stands for, so you can discover these important steps.

- **Recognize the emotion**
- **Understand the emotion**
- **Label the emotion**
- **Express the emotion**
- **Regulate the emotion**

Let's say, for example, you're at school and *you're about to take a test that you forgot to study for…*

1. The first step is to RECOGNIZE your emotions.

- As you enter the class, you can feel your body slouching, you become silent and your face shows that something terrible has happened. Your body is giving you clues about the state of your emotions.

2. Next, you need to UNDERSTAND your emotions.

- You are becoming more and more mindful and aware of your emotion. That helps you understand your emotions, your mood, and your reaction to it.

- You say to yourself something like, "I can't believe I forgot about the test! I know I'm feeling this way because I'm completely unprepared. I could fail!"

3. The next step is to LABEL the emotion.

- Go deeper than just "happy" or "sad." Dr. Marc Brackett suggests using a tool his team created called the "Mood Meter." Check it out at this link: https://www.marcbrackett.com/the-colors-of-our-emotions/. The Mood Meter helps us develop our emotional literacy and increase our vocabulary when communicating about emotions. This allows us to understand and communicate to others the very essence of what we are feeling.[6]

- You say to yourself something like, "I am so stressed and mad at myself for forgetting about the test. I am starting to panic, and I can't think straight."

4. Next, EXPRESS the emotion.

- By expressing our emotions, we put the emotion in the forefront of the entire experience and bring importance to the "feeling" side of life. It also allows us to consider how best to manage or regulate the emotions.

- You say to yourself something like, "I'm going to let my best friend know I forgot all about the test, and I'm a wreck about it. I'm also going to quickly text my mother and let her know... even though I know she will be mad."

5. Finally, REGULATE the emotion.

- Even though you're amped up, you can still take steps to calm yourself down. You can regulate your emotions. When you're mindful of your emotions and thoughts, you can make the best decision under stressful conditions.

- You say to yourself something like, "Let me first calm myself down... just take some slow, easy relaxing breaths... I will do the best that I can. I don't want to fail this test... that's not okay, but I have to make the best of it. I know I'll remember a lot of the material from my classes. All I can really do is try my best…. Ok, go for it!"

The example gives just a few things you can do to wisely manage your feelings, like using self-soothing or calming strategies. And try to not judge yourself too harshly! That helps you to think more clearly and helps you to make the best decisions. You can also use positive self-talk, like "I have to make the best of it" and "I do remember a lot of the material, I'll give it my best". By talking to yourself in a positive way, it gives you the best mindset to approach a difficult or stressful moment.[7]

There are many ways to help regulate your emotions. My advice is to come up with some emotional regulation strategies that work for you. It all starts with helping yourself achieve a calm mood and trying not to be too hard on yourself. Remember: your mind works best when it is calm. In general, you can try listening to music, call a friend, talk with your parents or a favorite teacher, do yoga or meditation, try something physical like a jog, take a good warm shower, etc. Whatever strategies you choose, they must work for you, and the strategies should support good mental health practices and not hurt you physically or emotionally. Also, each circumstance may call for different strategies depending on your preference, the time you have, and the setting you are in.

Follow the above "road map" and you are on your way to a healthy and successful emotional life!

7.3 – Discussion Questions

1. Who can help us think of some examples of situations that would be emotionally difficult for someone your age?

2. Next, let's pick one of these examples and apply each step of the RULER approach to managing our emotions. Remember, for each step we need to give ourselves permission to feel. Now, how can we complete each step?

- **Recognize the emotion –**

- **Understand the emotion –**

- **Label the emotion –**

- Express the emotion –

- Regulate the emotion –

Chapter 7 References

[1] Wechsler, D., Psychological Corporation., & Pearson Education, Inc. (2008). WAIS-IV: Wechsler Adult Intelligence Scale.

[2] Goleman, D., (1995) Emotional Intelligence, New York, NY, England: Bantam Books, Inc.

[3] "How to Turn Painful Emotions Into Superpowers." Psychology Today, 2020, https://www.psychologytoday.com/us/blog/midlife-matters/201811/how-turn-painful-emotions-superpowers.

[4] Brackett, Marc, Permission to Feel: Unlocking the Power of Emotions, Celadon Books, 2019

[5] Goleman, Daniel, Emotional Intelligence: Why It Can Matter More Than IQ, Bantam Books, 2006.

[6] Yale Center for Emotional Intelligence, RULER E.I. Training Institute, 2018.

[7] Mazza, James J., Dexter-Mazza, Elizabeth T., Miller, Alec L., Rathus, Jill H., Murphy, Heather E., DBT Skills in Schools, Skills Training for Emotional Problem Solving for Adolescents (DBT STEPS-A), The Guilford Press, 2016

Chapter 8

EMPATHY

8.1 – What is Empathy?

Hey, it's Tom again. Grab your phone. For real. I want to show you this three-minute video on **Empathy Vs. Sympathy** from one of my favorite researchers, Dr. Brené Brown. Here it is: https://youtu.be/1Evwgu369Jw.[1] You can also use your camera to scan the code on the right. The video starts with a commercial, so make sure to hit the SKIP button. I'll see you back here in three minutes. Ready… go.

Great video, right? **"Empathy is feeling _with_ people."** explains Dr. Brené Brown. That's exactly what the bear does for the fox. The bear displays the four qualities of empathy described earlier in the video. Look at the four qualities below, and ask yourself where each one is displayed in the video.

1. Perspective taking. We have to mentally put ourselves in the other person's shoes and try to see the problem from their point of view. That means "pressing pause" in our minds so we can be fully present and understand where they're coming from. **Questions for you:** At what point (or points) did the bear try to understand the perspective of the fox? When can perspective taking be difficult?

2. Staying out of Judgement. It's not our place to judge anyone (you already know that), but I don't think that's their main point. The main idea is about our tendency to either give advice or paint a "silver lining" around someone's pain. We want to help our friend – and that's a good thing – but if they're not asking for advice, we should NOT automatically jump in and try to solve the problem for them. Empathy includes acknowledging that we don't have all the answers. When we say things like "Here's what you should do…" we're actually making a judgement statement. When we say, "At least it's not as bad as…" we're actually minimizing their pain. **Questions for you:** Which character in the video was passing judgement and minimizing the fox's pain? What did the bear do (or NOT DO) to stay out of judgement?

3. Recognizing emotion in other people. This is the primary skill of empathy. If you watch closely, you can see the bear picking up on the fox's emotions all through the video, from start to finish. I counted at least five times, and maybe you can find more! **Questions for you:** How many times can you see the bear recognizing the fox's emotions? How would you describe the bear's attitude or demeanor as he hears about the fox's struggle?

4. Communicating their emotion back to them. The bear climbs down in the hole and says to the fox, "I know what it's like down here… and you're not alone." Notice how the bear does not go into a long story about all the past pain of the bear's life? That's important. To show empathy, we have to "go there" emotionally and show that we understand the other person's feelings, BUT… without making it all about us.

Empathy is About Them

Why do humans sometimes struggle with making it all about us? How can you communicate that you understand someone's emotions without saying you know **"exactly"** how they feel?

I like how Dr. Brown explains that people don't always want a solution:

> If I share something with you that's very difficult, I'd rather you say, **"Phew… I don't even know what to say right now… I'm just glad you told me."** Because the truth is: rarely can a response make something better. What makes something better is connection. – Dr. Brené Brown

When you show empathy, and when the other person opens up, it creates a deep personal connection between you. You're building trust. Think about how vulnerable the other person must feel to share their deepest feelings with you.

When a friend shares something deep with me, I automatically consider it confidential. I will never gossip or use that information against them. Trust is the foundation of all relationships.

But let me be clear. There are some situations where I am required to share information, especially if someone is in danger. Remember how I talked about mandatory reporting in chapter four? I hope you take on the same responsibility and get help for a friend if they've been abused or if someone is in danger.

Even if the other person begs you not to tell, you still need to do the right thing. Offer to go with your friend to talk with a trusted adult, like one of their parents or a counselor. After all, isn't **going there with them** what empathy is all about?

8.2 – The Science of Empathy

Hey y'all! It's your friendly neighborhood Dr. OH here to walk you through a little bit of the science of empathy, especially as it applies to your teenage years. Remember when we talked about Emotional Intelligence and how it relates to your brain in adolescence? We talked about the limbic system (where emotions happen in your brain) and the prefrontal cortex (where reasoning and decision-making happen). We discussed the fact that your prefrontal cortex is still developing, therefore your Emotional Intelligence is still developing.

So, where is empathy in this network between your emotional center and the reasoning center of the brain?

Originally, scientists proposed that the way our brain reacts when we experience emotions or pain is the same way it reacts when we see someone else experience emotions or pain. You see someone cry on TV and your brain mirrors what their brain is doing, so you get a little sad (or in my case, cry with them).

Turns out, this theory about brain activation during empathy is only partially true. To study the topic, scientists typically use the brain's pain pathways because we understand those pathways very well. This is the general research question: ***does the brain look the same when you experience pain directly versus when you see someone else experience pain?*** This is the general research answer: *yes and no*. In a review on the neuroscience of empathy, the authors use this example:

"Watching a needle puncture someone else's skin can be distressing, but it's not the same feeling as getting pricked yourself."[2]

Why does the brain behave this way? Because you understand that you exist separately from other people. Your brain doesn't stop taking that into account when you see other people experiencing emotions or pain. So, there is *some* overlap in activation – that's your brain saying, ***"I know how that feels."*** There are also areas of the brain that activate only when you experience an emotion ***directly***, and areas that activate only when you experience it ***vicariously*** (meaning through other people).

Because these brain regions are still going through so much change and development in your teenage years, your ability to be empathetic develops quite a bit during adolescence. In a longitudinal (meaning long-term) study on empathy, researchers tested a group of teenagers once a year for five years in a row, from age 12 to age 16. They found that empathy generally increased over the course of those five years.[3] They also found that the amount of increase varied significantly between individuals, and that girls generally had higher levels of empathy than boys. When the same teenagers turned 35 years old (like I said, it was a long study), they were tested again. This time, researchers found that the development of empathy during adolescence predicted how socially competent each individual was as an adult.

What does that mean? It means empathy is a key factor in all aspects of your social life. Do you want to relate to other people and be less awkward in social situations? You'll need empathy for that!

In another longitudinal study, 467 teens took a test to measure their empathy once a year starting at 13 years old.[4] This time, researchers found that adolescents typically displayed 1 of 3 levels of empathy: low, medium, or high.

Those with low levels of empathy, showed a ***decrease*** in empathy skills as they got older. Those with medium or high levels of empathy showed ***increases*** in empathy skills. This result reveals that not every adolescent is on the same developmental path – an important reminder that we are all different and our paths are not predetermined.

There has also been a line of research focused on where our level of empathy comes from in the first place. How did the teens with low, medium, or high empathy levels get to those levels? Turns out, there seem to be quite a few connections between the way that we are parented when we are young and how our empathy, conscience, and moral values develop.

When parents help their kids with reasoning about their decisions, they are more likely to have a better grasp of other peoples' perspectives when they get older. For example, "Lina is crying. Why do you think she's crying? You took her toy, and it's not nice to take someone's toy without asking." Those kinds of thought processes help a child develop empathy.[5]

For a discussion of more research on moral development, which includes empathy, have a look at the research by Dr. Nancy Eisenberg.[6] You can do a basic web search for "Dr. Nancy Eisenberg - Emotion, Regulation, and Moral Development" or if you're using an e-reader you can click on the link in the references at the end of this chapter.

You can also look at any of the articles in this section for more information. Those articles all have reference sections too, which can open up a whole world of information you never knew you needed to know. Have fun doing your research, and most importantly, have fun developing your empathy skills!

8.2 – Discussion Questions

1. What are some specific ways the skill of empathy can help you out in social situations?

2. Research has shown that women generally have higher levels of empathy than men. This does not mean all women have more than all men, but when you look at the averages, women score higher. Why do you think that is true?

3. Do you think you're a high, medium, or low empathy person? Why?

4. What are some ways we can try build our empathy skills?

8.3 – How to Increase Your Empathy Skills

Hi, its Dr. Kagan again. So now that you *totally* understand what empathy is, all you have to do is now be more empathetic and understanding! How difficult is that? If you catch my sarcasm here… it's really not that easy. It's hard to know what it feels like to *"walk a mile in someone else's shoes."*[7] Tom and Dr. OH already discussed what empathy is and how it works in your brain. Now I want to give you some practical tips for developing your empathy skills. For me, empathy is the very essence of or central to being human. But even I, a psychologist who is always supposed to be empathetic, have lapses of empathy.

Let me share a quick story with you. I was seeing four 8th grade students together in a weekly group counseling session at a middle school where I used to work. The purpose of the group was to help the students adjust to school and feel better about themselves. I led them through all kinds of activities that involved sharing feelings and building trust, so the group of boys would become more comfortable talking with me and with each other. I wanted them to feel open enough to share their positive and negative experiences in school.

Weeks went by and no matter what I tried I could sense and feel that the students were reluctant to talk about things. They usually said everything was fine or there were no issues to discuss. One student even suggested there was no need to meet weekly. I wasn't convinced there was nothing to talk about, so finally I asked what was wrong. I appealed to them to be open and honest, assuring them we would keep our conversations confidential.

What finally got expressed was the boys didn't feel comfortable with me. They felt that I wouldn't understand their issues. They shared that they were Black and

Latino, and I was White. And due to our different races and cultures, I never would be able to understand their experiences in school and in the community, and I wouldn't be able to empathize with their challenges and difficulties.

I had to do some deep, personal reflecting on how these young men perceived me. I also had to look at my own feelings about them not trusting me. I did feel hurt. I felt like a failure. You see, I needed to own this. In this moment, I failed to be empathetic. I had to work through that.

Most importantly, I needed to understand their experiences and perspectives and genuinely show that I understood them, so they could relate to me. Once the boys were able to voice their feelings and views, and once I listened with empathy (taking time to understanding their issues and perspectives), then our hearts and minds met, and we started working together to support their emotional needs.

This experience reminds me of a quote from our 26th president, Theodore Roosevelt. He said, **"No one cares how much you know until they know how much you care."** [8] That's the key: once the boys knew how much I cared about them, then they were able to open up and be real with me. So, let me share what I learned from this important experience by giving you the five insights below:

5 Tips for Developing Empathy

1. **Listen with your full attention.** Empathy is about understanding each other's perspective. The only way to understand each other's perspective is to listen. Sometimes the best thing I can do is to listen and shut up.

2. **Don't judge.** Try to be less judgmental, and honor other people's opinions (even if you disagree with them). Nothing shuts people down quicker than the feeling of being judged.

3. **Be aware of your own feelings.** When you're aware of your own emotions, it gives you a clearer perspective, and it helps you remain open to the thoughts and feelings of others.

4. **Don't be defensive.** You don't always have to defend yourself, argue your point and be right. That's much too much stress, and it makes it hard to be empathetic.

5. **Practice makes… progress!** Try and practice empathy. It's amazing! It feels wonderful when you say, "I hear you" and you know the other person really believes you. Or how terrific it is when you know a family member or friend "has your back". They have empathy for you. When you show empathy, it shows you care. As humans, empathy is the key skill that brings us together. It gives you a sense of connection, and it is incredibly rewarding.

Empathy is something we always have to work on, and no one is perfect at it. We can be understanding in some situations and not in others. You may have to take some time to process what they're really saying and communicating, so you can better understand their feelings. As you develop that sense of awareness, you will be able to show your empathetic self!

8.3 – Discussion Questions

1. Think about someone who showed empathy or was empathetic to you. Do you remember the situation or circumstances? How did it feel? What did they do that connected with you?

2. Can you think of a situation or circumstances where you were empathetic? How did you show your empathy?

3. Take a look at the boat metaphor from the beginning of the book. How can the skill of empathy fit in with the metaphor? (Remember: all metaphors eventually break down if we push the meaning too far.)

4. What could our school community do to emphasize more empathy?

5. What is one specific aspect of empathy you want to work on in your life?

Chapter 8 References

[1] The RSA. (2013). Brené Brown on Empathy. https://youtu.be/1Evwgu369Jw.

[2] McCall, C., & Singer, T. (2013). Empathy and the Brain. Understanding Other Minds: Perspectives from Developmental Social Neuroscience, Chapter 195-213.

[3] Allemand, M., Steiger, A. E., & Fend, H. A. (2015). Empathy Development in Adolescence Predicts Social Competencies in Adulthood. Journal of Personality, 83(2), 229-241. https://onlinelibrary.wiley.com/doi/abs/10.1111/jopy.12098

[4] Van Lissa, C. J., Hawk, S. T., De Wied, M., Koot, H. M., Van Lier, P., & Meeus, W. (2014). The Longitudinal Interplay of Affective and Cognitive Empathy Within and Between Adolescents and Mothers. Developmental Psychology, 50(4), 1219.

[5] Zahn-Waxler, C., Radke-Yarrow, M., & King, R. A. (1979). Child Rearing and Children's Prosocial Initiations Toward Victims of Distress. Child Development, 319-330.

[6] Eisenberg, N. (2000). Emotion, Regulation, and Moral Development. Annual Review of Psychology.

[7] Walking a Mile In Their Shoes- Great Quotes on Empathy, Mind Fuel Daily, August 2020, https://www.mindfueldaily.com/livewell/walking-a-mile-in-their-shoes-great-quotes-on-empathy/.

[8] "Quote of the Day", Good News Network, April 2020, https://www.goodnewsnetwork.org/theodore-roosevelt-quote-about-reputation/

Chapter 9

BASIC HUMAN NEEDS

9.1 – Maslow's Hierarchy of Needs

Hey everyone, Dr. Kagan here. As a teen, you've probably found yourself thinking about deep topics like: what do you want in life, what's important to you, and what do you need? Do you want to make a difference? Do you want to have a good job or be rich when you grow older? Do you want to be a professional athlete or a popular YouTuber? Do you want to be a doctor, a musician, or even president of the United States? Do you want to just be finished with school, and move out of your hometown? Maybe you want a family in your future. Or maybe you want to travel the world. Perhaps you want more happiness, confidence, and contentment. Or maybe you want less stress and anxiety and pain? Whatever your dreams are, they come from a deep place inside you.

Researchers, scientists, and mental health professionals have thought about and studied these questions. What do we want and need in life? What motivates us? And how do each of us establish life goals? Interestingly, when you were younger your parents or caregivers knew or assumed what you needed and took care of those needs for you. They fed you, gave you shelter and care, a place to sleep, loved you, scheduled your days and organized your fun and responsibilities. Now that you're older, you take more responsibility for taking care of your needs. By the time you reach your teen years, your needs can be quite complex.

Dr. Abraham Maslow, a famous researcher in the field of psychology,[1] organized needs into a pyramid which forms a hierarchy of five basic human needs that each person must achieve and master to live a full and complete life.[2] It's called "**Maslow's Hierarchy of Needs**," and it helps us understand our basic needs, motivation, and behavior. Let's take a look at the first level on the next page.

Maslow's Hierarch of Needs

- **Physical Needs** – The first layer at the bottom of the pyramid represents our most basic needs in life: our physical needs like food, water, sleep, shelter, and all our bodily functions including breathing, digestion, excretion, and even our sexual needs. Once these needs are satisfied, we can move up the hierarchy to more complex needs.

- **Safety Needs** – After our physical needs are met, we naturally pursue our safety needs which include: feeling safe and secure, being in a safe environment, and feeling protected from harm. Recently, there have been many worries and our feelings of safety have been really shaken. Many of us have experienced a lot of anxiety in life. Some parents have lost jobs or worry about job security because of the struggling economy. There is social unrest and tensions between different communities and segments of our population, and some communities are suffering more than others. The feeling that these problems must be solved, that's an example of our Safety Needs.

- **Social Needs** – As we climb the hierarch of needs, we discover our social needs for finding connection with other people. This involves feeling like we belong, feeling love and compassion for others, and welcoming others into our lives. At this level, many teens experience the importance of friendships, the beginning of intimate relationships, and welcoming others into their lives in a very deep and meaningful way.

- **<u>Esteem Needs</u>** – Still higher up the pyramid is the need of esteem, our need to feel that we are uniquely valuable and important. Naturally, this includes our self-esteem, but it also includes our need to feel esteemed and valued by others. This is where our true mature confidence emerges, and we begin to believe in ourselves with genuine self-esteem.

- **Self-Actualization** – As our lower level needs are met, can begin to experience the highest level of the pyramid – the need for Self-Actualization. It includes the deep sense that life is meaningful and pleasurable. This is where you experience contentment and genuine self-acceptance. It's the source of your creativity, your ambition, your empathy, problem solving, and the highest level of thinking.

Why is Maslow's Hierarchy of Needs such an important concept? Because the higher we go up the pyramid, the more fulfilled we feel in life. It shines a light on the fact that your needs are complex. During stressful times, your needs can feel very overwhelming and challenging. Maslow's Hierarchy of Needs can help us organize our thinking about ourselves and others.[3]

9.1 – Discussion Questions

1. How can Maslow's Hierarchy of Needs help us to better understand ourselves and our behavior?

2. How can the hierarchy help us understand the needs and behaviors of others?

3. What are some of your needs and desires? Can you pinpoint where each need fits in the Hierarchy of Needs? For example, perhaps hanging out with your friends on the weekend is very important to you. Try to identify as many needs as you can and discuss where they fit in the hierarchy.

9.2 – Self-Actualization

As we understand our needs, we can better take care of ourselves, establish personal goals and strategies, and achieve our life goals and ambitions. This can be such an important source of motivation for us. It can inspire us to problem solve, plan, and execute strategies that will meet those needs. Next, it helps us understand that other people will have different types of needs than we do, especially at the higher levels of the pyramid. As we understand and accept our differences, it helps us become more tolerant, patient, and accepting for everyone around us. It can also help you look at the maddening, annoying, frustrating aspects of being a teen and understanding that what is important to you and others should be valued, honored, and respected.

Self-Actualization is at the top of Maslow's Hierarchy of Needs for a reason.[4] It represents the highest need or level we can all achieve in our life. It includes feeling genuine self-acceptance, finding meaning and contentment in our life, having

ambition, empathy, and achieving our highest potential. To relate to this highest level, think of someone in your life, a role model, who you look up to or you would like to meet. That someone shows confidence, great acceptance and tolerance, creativity, empathy, wisdom, and love. It is probably someone older than you because to achieve all these wonderful attributes it takes many years of learning, growing and living life. For me, that's Mahatma Gandhi. He was an activist who through nonviolent resistance fought for India's independence and inspired freedom for all. I think of **self-actualization** as an aspiration or a strong desire (or hope) to become the very best version of yourself and to make a positive impact in the world.[5] Most of us do not fully achieve our aspirations. No one is perfect, but we can work toward our dreams and feel great satisfaction putting in the effort and achieving important goals or milestones along the way. So, what steps can you take in your journey toward **self-actualization**?

- Accept yourself and find humor in your own mistakes
- Don't be so quick to judge others

- Have a "creative spirit" and be willing to try new skills

- Develop meaningful relationships

- See the goodness in life and stay positive

- Accept problems and become a good problem solver

- Show empathy and compassion for others

- Choose enjoyable and meaningful goals for your life

Of course, climbing to the higher levels of Maslow's hierarchy will sometimes be thwarted by things out of our control. Think about the boat metaphor. When you're boating, you might have severe weather which may force you to temporarily abort your journey or take a detour. Life can be challenging and unpredictable like that.

Fortunately, there are many choices you can make along the way – choices that you can control. Whether you steer into a storm or steer away from a storm is in your control. Making good choices to be your best self and live a meaningful, positive life is in your control.

Over the course of time, positive choices will steer your life toward self-actualization, fulfillment, and becoming the best version of yourself. That's the ultimate goal!

9.2 – Discussion Questions

1. Break into small groups of three or four students per group. Assign one person to be the drawer. This person should take out a fresh piece of paper and do a quick sketch of Maslow's Hierarchy (make sure to add the names of the levels). Next, assign someone to be the writer. Now, brainstorm as a group and come up with at least four needs for each level of the pyramid. Ready? Set. Go!

2. Now let's take a minute and have each group report back, listing at least two needs from each of the five levels. Which group would like to go first?

3. If you were having a difficult time understanding someone's behavior (let's say someone was rude to you earlier in the day, and now you're at home thinking about it), how could you use Maslow's Hierarchy of Needs to have more mental empathy for them?

Chapter 9 Personal Reflection Journal

Take a few minutes to journal about how your needs have changed as you've grown older. What obstacles or circumstances have gotten in the way of having your needs met? How did you overcome those obstacles? Do you think your needs will continue to change over time? How so?

Chapter 9 References

[1] Maslow, A.H., *A Theory of Motivation*, Martino Publishing, 2013, Reprint of 1943 Edition.

[2] Abraham Maslow. Wikipedia, 2020. From https://en.wikipedia.org/wiki/Abraham_Maslow.

[3] The 5 Levels of Maslow's Hierarchy of Needs by Kendra Cherry, VeryWellMind.com, June 2020. https://www.verywellmind.com/what-is-maslows-hierarchy-of-needs-4136760.

[4] Self-Actualization", Good Therapy, March 2019. From https://www.goodtherapy.org/learn-about-therapy/issues/self-actualization.

[5] Maslow's Hierarchy of Needs by Saul McLeod, SimplyPsychology.com, March 2020. https://www.simplypsychology.org/maslow.html.

Chapter 10

SELF-CARE

10.1 – What is Self-Care?

Hey everybody! It's Dr. Kirleen, back to talk about self-care. This term is thrown around so often that the real definition gets lost along the way. Self-care has become a trendy buzzword for getting a manicure or buying yourself something nice. While I love a good mani-pedi, true self-care is so much more.

Self-care is any activity you do deliberately to take care of your mental, emotional, and physical health. It means giving yourself the same grace, compassion, and care that you give to others.

Although self-care is a simple concept, it's something we very often overlook because many of us were taught to put the needs of others ahead of our own. I do believe giving is a virtue, but I do not buy into the message that this means we have to live a life spent ignoring our own needs.[1]

A few years ago, I learned this lesson the hard way. I found myself being tired all the time and irritated with everyone and everything. I realized that I had forgotten to stop and do what would help me recharge and bring me joy.

Now, I'm so serious about self-care, I have a list in the notes section of my phone called "Joy Rising." The list is filled with different activities I do every week to take care of myself. Some of them are simple, like going for a morning walk. Others are complex, like journaling about the things I'm feeling.

Making **self-care** a part of my everyday life has made an enormous difference. Self-worth and self-care go hand in hand. Practicing self-care is a great way to maintain a healthy relationship with yourself. Regardless of what's going on at home, school, or with family, you deserve to practice self-care.[2]

Your Body's Talking. Listen.

If you are neglecting self-care, physical and mental symptoms can show up in your body. These symptoms can easily fly under the radar. Being irritable, feeling stressed or burned out, holding tension in areas of your body, experiencing aches and pains, and problems sleeping are common. These may seem like little things at the moment. So, we rarely stop to consider how we're caring for ourselves. If you notice you're becoming snappy with family or friends, if you're waking up at all hours of the night, or you're feeling physically and emotionally spent, you may be lacking self-care.

Take a look at this list and see if any of these sound like you.[3]

1. Your tolerance for people has reached an all-time low. You're reacting emotionally to feedback from teachers or parents or snapping at your friends for no reason.

2. Your sleep is out of whack. You can't fall asleep at night or are sleeping too much. Elevated stress during the day can create stress hormones in your body that make it more difficult to sleep at night.

3. You're struggling to manage your emotions. You're crying more frequently and feel angry, but you're not sure why.

4. You can't focus. Simple tasks or homework assignments are taking you longer to complete than usual, and you're making silly mistakes on homework or at home.

5. You're not enjoying anything you do. Activities you use to enjoy doing, like spending time with friends, seem like a chore.

6. You're routinely getting sick. You feel sick or like you have the flu, but nothing is wrong.

Take Time to Re-Charge

Self-care is all about rest, recovery, and recharging. Consider your smartphone. You plug it in all the time to charge it back to 100%. The question is: what are you doing to charge yourself back to 100%? You can't give people energy you don't have. If your battery is only charged to 20%, you can't give someone 30%.

In the boat metaphor, self-care is the fuel for the boat. When the boat is out of gas, you have to refuel. The same thing is true in life: when you're running low on energy, you have to rest and refill your tank.

Everything has to rest eventually. We sleep at night, summer turns into to fall, and even animals hibernate or lie dormant for periods. Everything in the universe needs time to rest and recover – even you. When you take time to rest, recover, and recharge, it helps you live your best life and be your best self.

10.1 – Discussion Questions

1. What is self-care? Why is it important?

2. What are some daily activities that use up a lot of mental energy?

3. Name a signal from your body that lets you know you need self-care.

4. What are some of the most effective and meaningful self-care activities you do to re-charge?

10.2 – 3 Steps to a Self-Care Plan

 Are you ready to take the next step and develop a self-care plan? Today I'm going to break it down for you in three important steps. But before you rush through the steps, you need to be mindful of your mental and physical experiences. You have to know what stresses you out, what brings you joy, and what coping mechanisms work best for you. Don't assume that what works for your friends will always work for you. Instead, take your time with each step below. Write out your thoughts for each section, or make journal entries, or draw if that works for you. Explore the three steps below, and take enough time to take the process seriously.[4]

1. Evaluate your current coping skills.

Examining your own habits is an important first step in developing a self-care plan. How do you typically deal with stress? When faced with challenges, we can use either positive coping strategies or negative coping strategies. Be honest when evaluating your current behaviors. If you find yourself lashing out, reaching for junk food, or shutting down, those are negative coping habits. Positive coping habits are things like pausing to take several deep breaths or refocusing your thoughts during periods of frustration.

2. Identify your self-care needs.

Take a moment to consider what you value and need in your everyday life (daily self-care needs) versus what you value and need in the event of a crisis (urgent self-care needs). For instance, one of my daily self-care needs is to have at least an hour of downtime where I can unwind and unplug. But when I'm in an urgent situation, I need to have contact with people I can express my thoughts and feelings with.

Remember that self-care extends far beyond your basic physical needs – consider your emotional, spiritual, social, and school needs. Once you've determined your daily needs and emergency needs, write them down.

3. Create your plan.

Your self-care plan can be as simple or complex as you need it to be. It's a good idea to keep a detailed plan at home and carry a simplified electronic version on your phone. Your plan should have positive coping strategies for daily self-care needs and urgent self-care needs.

Sometimes it's hard to really know ourselves and understand our self-care needs. If you're struggling with this topic, or if you don't know where to start, reach out to a trusted adult, such as your parents or a mental health professional for help.

10.2 – Discussion Questions

1. As you were reading through the three steps, which one stood out to you the most, and why?

2. What are some of the challenges or distractions that could get in the way of your self-care plan?

3. Take out a new sheet of paper. Using the three-step process discussed above (Evaluate, Identify, Create) create a self-care plan for yourself that includes emotional and physical components.

Chapter 10 References

[1] Lee, K. (2019, October 4). Self-Care Isn't Selfish or Superficial. Psychology Today. https://www.psychologytoday.com/us/blog/rethink-your-way-the-good-life/201910/self-care-isn-t-selfish-or-superficial

[2] "9 Signs You're Overdue for a Mental Health Day" Brit +Co. 2020. From https://www.brit.co/signs-its-time-to-take-a-mental-health-day/.

[3] "6 Subtle Signs You Are Overdue for Self-Care: Self-Care Is Not a Luxury!" The American Institute of Stress, 16 Oct. 2017, www.stress.org/self-care-is-not-a-luxury.

[4] Tygielski, Shelly, et al. "Why You Need a Self-Care Plan." Mindful, 28 May 2019, www.mindful.org/why-you-need-a-self-care-plan/.

Chapter 11

HEALTHY LIVING

11.1 – Take Care of Your Body

Hey everybody, it's Tom again. It's a silly old saying, but there's some truth to it: *you are what you eat.* Your body runs on the fuel you give it, and that means your food, drinks, vitamins, and any prescribed medications you take. Here's the key takeaway: your fuel has a HUGE impact on your mental health. As a teen, you should already know that sugary and fatty foods like soda, candy, and donuts can never give your body the kind of pure nutrition it needs. Obviously, nutrition comes from natural foods like fruits, vegetables, and proteins. If you want your body and brain to operate together in harmony, you have to fill it with the right types (and amounts) of fuel.

This topic might seem like something only adults need to worry about, but nutrition is SUPER IMPORTANT during your teen years. Your bones, brain, and body are still developing, and they need proper nutrients to grow at a healthy rate.[1] Experts say that healthy eating is the number one factor for maintaining the right weight for your body type (yes, even more than physical exercise). Eating healthy also reduces your risk for diseases like diabetes, heart disease, and high blood pressure.[2] The habits you form as a teen will follow you into adulthood, so it's really important to start now. Don't put it off.

A Framework for Healthy Eating

If you really want to eat healthy, you need some basic guidelines that are based on science. That's where the **MyPlate** plan comes in. MyPlate is a simple guide developed by the U.S. Department of Agriculture. It helps you make healthy food choices based on the five basic food groups. The best part is: it's visual and easy to remember. You can dig deeper on their site at https://ChooseMyPlate.gov,[3] or you can let me break it down for you on the next page. Come on now…

1. **Vegetables**, like salad, peas, carrots, broccoli, and cucumber.

2. **Fruits**, like apples, bananas, pears, peaches, and watermelon.

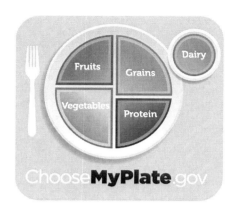

3. **Grains**, like breads and pasta. Try to eat whole grains, like whole-wheat bread, rice, or oatmeal. They're less processed and healthier for you.

4. **Protein**, like meat, fish, beans, nuts.

5. **Dairy**, like milk, cheese, and yogurt.

Half your plate should be full of fruits and veggies (with more veggies than fruit). Grains and protein should each take up about a quarter of your plate. Then, add a small side of dairy, and boom – you're balanced. Eating three healthy meals a day – including breakfast – helps stabilize your blood sugar and keeps you feeling alert and energized all day long.

Establishing Healthy Habits

Having a balanced plate is a great first step, but you also want to think about what you're eating throughout the rest of the day. When you're snacking between meals or after dinner (yes, I do it too) remember to reach for the fruits and veggies or just grab a glass of ice water.[4] Sometimes you're merely dehydrated, my friend. (talking to myself again, sigh…).

Here's another great tip that has really helped me and my family. When we're eating, we put away the screens – no phones at the table. Meals are a great time to connect with friends and family, or if you're eating alone, put on some music or listen to a podcast. Research shows that eating in front of a screen makes you more likely to overeat (and again, I know from experience, sigh…).

A Note About Dieting

Nutrition is a key part of overall health, but it's important not to confuse healthy eating with extreme dieting. Creating and practicing healthy habits is great, but restricting your food intake can be harmful, and it can even make you gain more weight in the future. (Yikes!) The diet culture you see on TV or online – with a focus on fast weight-loss – has been proven to be harmful for kids and teens.[5]

If you're concerned about your body size or your eating habits, reach out to a trusted adult like a parent, guardian, or your family doctor. It's important to make decisions that are right for your body.

Eating My Stress Away

Okay, confession time: This is embarrassing, but many times I've found myself using food as a source of coping with stress and anxiety. Sometimes I use food as a way of rewarding myself for a hard days' work. ***You deserve it, Tommy-T!*** (I guess that's what I'm thinking subconsciously.) And then the next morning I regret it every time. Here's what I've noticed: I'm more likely to slip into this behavior at the end of the day when I'm tired or watching screens.

Thankfully, my wife Casie helps me stay healthy. We're a team! We buy healthy, fresh groceries (along with a few sweets and snacks). And when one of us is weak, the other is strong. Obviously, you're not married yet, so find a family member or a friend to help keep you accountable. It really works.

Over the years I've realized that I'm not a weirdo, and a lot of people have similar weaknesses with food. I've also learned to give myself some grace because for one: **I'm working on it**, for two: **I know I'll never be perfect**, and for three: **it's never too late to start over.**

What about you? What are your strengths and weaknesses when it comes to food? What else are you eating and drinking and consuming? How is it affecting your body and your mind? The more you think about it, the more you'll see how it impacts your mental health.

11.1 – Discussion Questions

1. Can you think of any popular diets that disagree with the MyPlate model?
2. How do your typical meals compare to the MyPlate model?
3. Do you think it is possible for unhealthy eating to become a form of self-hate or self-harm? Why or why not?
4. How can healthy eating be a form of self-care?

11.2 – Me and My Treadmill Desk

One of the best investments I ever made in my physical health was purchasing a treadmill-desk. Yes, I actually own a standup desk with a treadmill underneath it. And yes, I'm walking on it right now as I type this sentence. What I didn't know was: it was also an investment in my mental health. Walking at a nice slow pace of about 2 to 2 ½ miles-per-hour keeps me alert and helps me stay focused.

I know you probably can't afford a treadmill desk as a teen, and I'm not telling you to get one. I'm just saying we all need to ask ourselves, "What else can I do to invest in my physical health, and in doing so, invest in my mental health?" We've got to make exercise a natural part of our daily routine, or it won't happen.

Check your phone stats and compare your active time to your screen time. Yesterday, did you spend more time on your phone or being active? No shame, and I don't claim to be the perfect example here, but it's true: a huge part of the population has replaced their active time with screen time.

A recent study found that teens are averaging over **SEVEN HOURS** of screen time per day just on entertainment alone. And that number does not include time spent using the phone for school. That means today's teens are using their phones **MORE THAN TWICE AS MUCH** as four years ago.[6]

And yes, I am yelling **WHEN I USE ALL CAPS**. But I'm yelling in a spirit of love because I'm trying to give you a wakeup call. It's time to do a reality check.

Our bodies were made to move, but our culture often requires us to sit. In school you're expected to sit down, sit up, sit still, and scooch over all the time. You are required to spend a lot of time on our butt, and that's not your fault.

Your fault – or your responsibility – is what you do with the rest of your free time: before school, on the bus, in-between classes, after school, after dinner, and on the weekends. That's when you have to get up and get moving!

There's no arguing with the facts on this one: science has proven time and again that people who are physically active live longer and have lower risk for diseases like depression and diabetes… and even some cancers.

Set a Daily Movement Goal

As a teen I had severe allergies and asthma (I still do), so I couldn't run for more than a minute without having an asthma attack. My inhaler was basically my best friend. I knew the needs of my body, so I had to find low-impact, low heart-rate activities to stay active.

I walked, rode my bike, went hiking, went swimming, rode my skateboard (barely), and… I even went rollerblading (don't judge).

My wife, Casie, loves doing yoga, zumba, and pretty much anything where people dance on a screen. What about you? What are your favorite activities? And more importantly, how much exercise are you getting?

The American Heart Association recommends that teens get a minimum of 60 minutes of moderate to vigorous exercise every day. Moderate is more my speed, as you know, but go vigorous if your body can take it!

According to the American College of Cardiology, only about 20% of teens get enough daily exercise.[7] If you're not getting an hour a day, don't beat yourself up. Challenge yourself to make a weekly exercise plan, and add reminders in your phone, so it alerts you when it's time to get up and get moving.

Teens who get consistent exercise have healthier bodies, are less likely to be depressed, and they even have improved cognitive function. That's right, exercise can even make you smarter (or at least unleash the potential you already have!).

Exercise Helps You Reset Your Mind

We always hear about the physical benefits of exercise, but what about the mental health benefits? Exercise helps your mind refresh itself when you're feeling moody or even depressed. It helps you reset when you're feeling stuck, and it's a great way to boost your attitude.

Research has shown that being active as a teen is linked with being happier as an adult.[8] (So get off the couch and get moving!)

If you want double bang for your buck, join a sports team. You'll get all of the exercise plus a sense of belonging, teamwork, and collaboration. Hopefully you'll become close friends with some of your teammates, and they will become part of your support system.

So, what are you waiting for? Get off your butt and get moving! Make a weekly exercise plan with a friend or a sibling, and keep each other accountable to stick with it! You got this.

11.2 – Discussion Questions

1. Why do you think so few teens get the recommended amount of exercise?

2. What are some ways you can get more exercise in your normal daily routine, but without spending any money at all? (For example, without buying any special equipment or joining a gym.)

3. What kinds of barriers might prevent people from getting enough exercise, even when they know it's important?

4. Picture this: it's been a long day. You're feeling tired, depressed, or even angry, but then you force yourself to get up and get moving. What kinds of things start to happen in your brain and in your attitude?

11.3 – The Science of Sleep

 Hey y'all! Dr. OH here to talk about snoozing. Personally, I love it. I'm really good at it, and if I don't get enough of it, I mutate into something really scary and very cranky. But all joking aside, sleep is a **critical** part of maintaining your physical health and your mental health.

The Brain During Sleep

To understand why sleep is so important, we need to talk a little bit about how it works. There are 4 stages of sleep. which can be identified by the pattern of electricity produced by your brain in each stage. Remember when we talked about how neurons communicate with electrical signals? The pattern produced by a repeating series of these electrical signals is called a **brainwave**. Researchers can see what stage of sleep a person is in by measuring their brainwaves with a device called an **electroencephalogram (EEG)** that looks like a swimming cap with a bunch of little suction cups on it. The "suction cups" are actually sensors called electrodes that measure the electrical impulses happening in your head. Because of this kind of cool technology, we also know that you cycle through each of your 4 sleep stages several times a night.

Let's talk about the last stage first. Stage 4 is called **Rapid Eye Movement**, or **REM**, sleep. This is the stage of your dreams. Literally — your brain produces activity that you perceive as dreams. When you're in REM sleep, there is so much activity going on in your brain that EEG waves look very similar to when you're awake. As the name of the stage implies, your eyes and eyelids move and flutter rapidly during REM sleep. Your body also paralyzes itself during REM, which sounds scary, but it's really for your protection. The paralysis keeps you from physically acting out your dreams as you sleep (sleepwalking, for example). The REM stage of sleep typically lasts anywhere from 10 minutes to 1 hour.

The first three stages of sleep are called **non-rapid-eye-movement stages (non-REM).** The first non-REM stage lasts anywhere from 5-10 minutes, and it's kind of like dozing. The second stage lasts a bit longer (10-25 minutes) and is a light sleep. The third non-REM stage is the deep sleep phase. This is the really restful stage when your body gets a chance to repair damage and prepare itself for the next day. You can go to www.sleepfoundation.org for more on the stages of sleep.

You Sleep; Your Brain Doesn't

For as much experience as we all have sleeping, scientists are still trying to answer questions about what happens while we sleep. One thing we do know is that your brain is definitely not sleeping while you sleep.

There is plenty of evidence that suggests that the brain is performing a task called **memory consolidation** as you sleep. Consolidation is a process of combining bits of information into a solid, meaningful, whole concept. In terms of memory, the phrase "bits of information" refers to the new experiences and knowledge that you encounter over the course of a day.

As you sleep, the brain takes the most valuable information bits, puts them together, and makes them available for long-term use. One study found that when people are forced to stay up all night after learning a difficult task, they lose most of what they learned.[9] Lots of other studies have used different methods and have come to the same conclusion. Which means that pulling those all-nighters before your exams is probably not a good idea!

Sleep is also important for things other than memory. When a person is deprived of a few hours of sleep for just a few nights in a row, they start having trouble in areas like:

- **Mental acuity:** Acuity means sharpness. Being mentally sharp helps with tasks like learning, thinking, planning, and self-control.

- **Reaction time:** This is how long it takes for you to react to a situation. Reaction time is really important for quickly avoiding danger. It also comes in handy for sports (and mosquito swatting if you live in Texas).

- **General physical health:** When you don't sleep, you get tired. Long-term physical fatigue can lead to reduced activity, which we know causes a host of different health problems, including obesity, heart, and blood pressure issues.

- **Mental health:** This whole book is about mental health…and sleep is important for all of it.

How much sleep is enough sleep?

The minimum amount of sleep you need depends on what stage of your life you are in. The National Sleep Foundation[10] recommends different amounts of sleep for different age groups:

- 0-3 months old: 14-17 hours

- 4-11 months old: 12-15 hours

- 1-2 years old: 11-14 hours

- 3-5 years old: 10-13 hours

- 6-13 years old: 9-11 hours

- 14-17 years old: 8-10 hours

- 18-64 years old: 7-9 hours

- 65+ years old: 7-8 hours

Of course, these are recommendations based on the **average** amount of sleep needed in each of these phases of life. But you are not an average – you are a unique person. That means that you might need more or less than the average hours of sleep for your age in order to function at your best. You'll know if you're not getting the sleep you need if you start having problems in the areas we just talked about – mental acuity, reaction time, physical health, and mental health.

If you have ongoing problems falling asleep and/or staying asleep, that's called **insomnia**, and you should definitely talk with your doctor or a mental health professional. Many people are prescribed medications or over-the-counter supplements, like melatonin, for sleep. Melatonin is the hormone your body releases as you drift off to sleep. The point is: if you're struggling with sleep, talk with your doctor.

For more information on the importance of sleep and how sleep deprivation can affect you, see Stanley Coren's book, *Sleep Thieves.*[11] And in the meantime, sweet dreams, y'all!

11.3 – Discussion Questions

1. How much sleep do you personally need to be at your best?

2. What happens to you when you don't get enough sleep?

3. If you were having ongoing trouble falling asleep or staying asleep, what would you do about it?

4. Are there ways that technology can potentially help or hurt your sleep? Explain your thoughts. Remember, it's not a debate, we're just sharing ideas and possibilities.

5. **Sleep Journal Challenge:**

    Keep a sleep journal for one week. Sometimes taking notes and looking at the big picture can help you spot weak points in your sleep habits. Keep track of the following:

    * Steps of your bedtime routine

    * The time you got in bed

    * How long you think it took to fall asleep

    * Number of times you awoke in the night

    * The time you awoke in the morning

    * Details of any dreams you had

Chapter 11 References

[1] Johns Hopkins Medicine. Healthy Eating During Adolescence. 2020. From https://www.hopkinsmedicine.org/health/wellness-and-prevention/healthy-eating-during-adolescence.

[2] Centers for Disease Control and Prevention. Physical Activity. 2020. From https://www.cdc.gov/healthyplaces/healthtopics/physactivity.htm.

[3] United States Department of Agriculture. What is My Plate? 2020. From https://www.choosemyplate.gov/eathealthy/WhatIsMyPlate.

[4] U.S. Department of Health and Human Services. Importance of Good Nutrition. 2020. From https://www.hhs.gov/fitness/eat-healthy/importance-of-good-nutrition/index.html.

[5] Boston Children's Hospital. How is Diet Culture Affecting Me? 2020, From https://youngwomenshealth.org/wp-content/uploads/2018/09/How-is-Diet-Culture-Affecting-Me.pdf.

[6] Jacobo, J. (2019, October 29). Teens Spend More Than 7 Hours On Screens For Entertainment A Day. ABC News. https://abcnews.go.com/US/teens-spend-hours-screens-entertainment-day-report/story?id=66607555.

[7] American College of Cardiology. Physical Activity Guidelines for Americans. 2020. From https://www.acc.org/latest-in-cardiology/ten-points-to-remember/2018/11/14/14/37/the-physical-activity-guidelines-for-americans.

[8] Sabitson, Catherine. Why Kids In Team Sports Become Happier Adults. 2020. From https://www.anxiety.org/team-sports-help-teens-avoid-depression.

[9] Stickgold, R., Malia, A., Maguire, D., Roddenberry, D., & O'Connor, M. (2000). Replaying the Game: Hypnagogic Images in Normals and Amnesics. Science, 290(5490), 350-353.

[10] Suni, E. (July, 2020). How Much Sleep Do We Really Need? National Sleep Foundation - SleepFoundation.org. Retrieved from https://www.sleepfoundation.org/articles/how-much-sleep-do-we-really-need.

[11] Coren, S. (1997). *Sleep Thieves*. Simon and Schuster.

Chapter 12

SUPPORT SYSTEMS

12.1 – Developing Your Support System

Hey everybody, it's Tom again. As a teen, it's easy to feel like you're the only one – the only person struggling socially or academically or relationally. You see everyone's amazing highlight reel on social media, and their lives seem perfect, but you never see the images they delete. The truth is: everyone has their own struggles, and we all need a solid support system to hold us up when we're falling down.[1] In the boat metaphor, struggles may feel like a storm or bad weather, but they can come from any combination of the elements in the metaphor, from **what you can control** to **what you can't**. When your life feels like a stranded boat in the middle of the ocean… in the middle of the night… and you're out of gas, and the boat it leaking, and the storm is raging… **who** and **what** do you turn to for help? That's your support system.[2]

5 Elements of Your Support System

1. People – We all need trusted people who love and support us no matter what. Who would you turn to if you were at your wit's end? **People are the most important aspect of your support system.**[3] We need mentors (lighthouses) who can guide us through our darkest night. We also need other people (other boats) to help us on the journey of life. These people can be friends, family members, teachers, counselors, or any trusted person you can talk to voice-to-voice. Write the names of the people in your support system below:

–

–

–

–

2. Places – We all need safe places where we can be fully ourselves without the fear of being hurt or judged. We need more than just physical safety; we need emotional safety, especially in moments of pain, fear, or anxiety. List some places you can go to feel safe:

–

–

–

3. Things – We need physical things in our support system. Obviously we need food, shelter, clothing, transportation, money, etc., but what other physical objects do you need for support? Maybe you have a favorite book or an app that helps you manage stress. Maybe you have a pet cat, or a favorite pillow, or a favorite pillow shaped like a cat. List some things that are supportive to you:

–

–

–

4. Beliefs – We all need some core beliefs and values to guide our decisions. What is important to you in life? What is true? I don't want to give examples here because I want you to think deeply about what you believe and list it below:

–

–

–

5. Activities – What are some activities or coping skills that help you refresh? What works best for you? What fills your tank? Try to list some activities that boost your energy, and some activities that help you calm down or unwind:

–

–

–

–

–

12.2 – Healthy Romantic Relationships

Hey guys! It's Dr. Kirleen back to talk about teen dating! Healthy romantic relationships can be part of your support system. As a teen, it's very normal to find yourself excited about the idea of dating a significant other. Counting the minutes until you see that person again, wondering what to wear, and beaming over a text message can all be beautiful experiences. But relationships are also complicated, so it's no surprise that things can go really right… or they can go really wrong.

In high school hallways and on social media, relationships are glamorized. Couples post their best photos and videos, and they look so in love. Seeing classmates with their boyfriend or girlfriend can make you long to have that same experience. This is a normal feeling; we all want to feel like someone likes us. But the seemly perfect love birds can give you a false sense of how difficult relationships can get.

When you consider getting into a romantic relationship (or breaking up), it's important to look at the whole picture, both the positives and the negatives, or as I call them, the Green Flags and the Red Flags. Let's start with the green flags for a healthy romantic relationship.

Six Relationship Green Flags

1. Good Communication. The foundation of all great relationships starts with good communication. You should be able to talk to each other and share feelings that are important to you, even if those feelings are unpleasant. Sometimes you may need a minute to think something through before you're ready to talk. The right person will give you space to think and not make you feel guilty for needing more time.

2. Giving Each Other Space. Healthy romantic relationships give each other space to spend time with family and friends. Before dating, you both had lives (families, friends, interests, hobbies, etc.), and that shouldn't change. Neither of you should give up seeing your friends or drop out of activities you love. You also should feel free to keep developing new talents, making new friends, and moving forward with life.

3. Respecting Emotional Boundaries. The person you date should get how great you are and respect your emotional boundaries. Emotional boundaries are the lines that separate your thoughts and feelings from those of other people. Violations of emotional boundaries look like someone telling you how to think and feel, blaming you for their mistakes, and pushing you to sacrifice your own needs.

4. Respecting Physical Boundaries. Setting boundaries around what each individual is comfortable with is crucial for a healthy relationship. Both parties should fully consent to any physical contact. Always remember you have the right to say what is okay and what's not okay. You should never feel pressured to go further than what you want with physical affection so make sure to be clear about your boundaries. You should be able to wear what you want, do what you want, and be who you want without worrying about your partner's reaction.

5. Handling Disagreements with Respect. Disagreements happen in every relationship and making sure you handle disputes with respect is key to having a healthy romantic relationship. If your partner resorts to name-calling or belittling you in any way, this is a red flag. In a healthy relationship, you should feel comfortable speaking your mind without being afraid of your partners reaction. You should also be open to listening and understanding your partner's perspective.

6. Healthy Digital Boundaries. In today's world, technology is a huge part of any teen relationship. It is essential to make sure technology isn't interrupting your day-to-day life to the point that it's disrupting your normal routine and family time.[4] You should never be pressured to send inappropriate pictures, share passwords, or feel like you have to post about your relationship status. Talk to your boyfriend or girlfriend about your expectations when it comes to digital boundaries, and make sure you're clear about it.

Six Relationship Red Flags

Now that we've taken a look at some of the green flags in teen relationships, it's important to look at the red flags. Red flags are signs that the relationship may be headed in an unhealthy direction, physically, emotionally, or mentally. These signs are vital to spot because one in three teens will experience physical or sexual abuse, or both.[5] Many times, these behaviors are used to gain power or control, and they can quickly escalate into violence or abuse.

1. Unpredictable Volatile Behavior. Everyone has a rough day once in a while, but unpredictable overreactions that make you feel like you need to walk on eggshells is not healthy. If your partner yells at you, intimidates you, threatening to hurt you, or destroy things you love, this is a huge red flag that the relationship is unhealthy.

2. Isolation. Keeping you away from friends, family, or other people you love is another red flag. Your partner should not make you choose between them or your friends. Insisting you spend all your time with them more than selfish; it's unhealthy.

3. Betrayal. Cheating, lying, and other deceptions are very hurtful and can leave you feeling heartbroken. Teen relationships have many ups and downs, but if you find yourself continually dealing with betrayal, this is a warning signal that your boat is in rough waters.

4. Deflecting Responsibility. If your partner is always blaming you, other people, or past experiences for their own actions, that's another red flag. In a healthy relationship, both parties can admit when they're wrong and apologize sincerely.

5. Manipulation. Manipulation is not always easy to spot, especially if you are new to dating. Some examples are pressuring or convincing you to do things that you wouldn't normally feel comfortable doing, ignoring you until you do what they want, and using gifts or fake apologies to pressure you to forgive their bad behavior.

6. Jealousy. An emotion that everyone experiences once in a while is jealousy, but if your partner lashes out or tries to control you because they are jealous, this is a problem. Jealousy can quickly escalate to violent behavior, so don't mistake jealousy for love.

Summary – Teen Romantic Relationships

Dating for the first time can take you to new highs – and new lows. You may find yourself on top of the world one day and feeling like you can't breathe the next. Learning how to spot unhealthy relationship patterns **(the red flags)** before they become too problematic is just as important as learning how to identify and develop the healthy patterns **(the green flags).** If you ever have a hard time getting out of a relationship, make sure to talk with your parents or a trusted adult about it right away, so they can help you make the right decision.

12.2 – Discussion Questions

1. Which of the 6 Red Flags (of unhealthy relationships) would you find the most alarming or hurtful to you?

2. Which of the 6 Green Flags (of healthy relationships) would feel the most meaningful or important to you?

3. If you felt trapped in an unhealthy romantic relationship, what would you do?

12.3 – Peer Pressure & Conformity

 Hi y'all! Dr. OH here. Sometimes our innate (built-in) need to be socially accepted causes us to follow the crowd – which can be a good thing or a bad thing. As humans, we tend to mimic and copy each other. Not in the annoying little sibling "STOP COPYING ME!" way. It's more like, "When I see someone crying, I get sad too." This is sometimes referred to as the Chameleon Effect, and it's an important aspect of empathy (which of course, is a fantastic skill). When we empathize with others, we are better able to communicate with them. Good communicators have more successful relationships, and who doesn't want successful relationships?

The downside to the Chameleon Effect is that we tend to sometimes mimic others without thinking about what we're doing. **We all experience moments of peer pressure in our lives when we feel compelled to conform with the group.** Conformity is all about going with the crowd and being part of the norm. Of course, this isn't always bad: if your friends are all going to a party dressed up in costumes, why shouldn't you do it too (if that's your thing)? The trouble begins when we start blindly following other people without thinking about what we're doing, why we're doing it, and whether it's the right thing to do.

Here's a question for you: in this drawing, which line on the right – **A**, **B**, or **C** – is the same length as the line on the left? Pretty easy answer, right? But what if peer pressure could influence you to pick a different answer? In a famous study done in the 1950s, Dr. Solomon Asch demonstrated the power of peer pressure by asking that same question to a group of people. Here's the tricky part of the

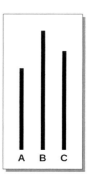

A B C

experiment: he put each person in a group with other seemingly random people… but they were not random at all! They were actually actors pretending to be participating in the experiment. In other words, only one person was a random participant, and the rest were fake. When the group was asked to choose the matching line, the actors all chose a line that was clearly not the correct answer. And get this: 75% of the time, the random participant person would end up conforming to the group by choosing an answer they knew was wrong! [6, 7]

Why would anyone do something so blatantly wrong just because other people are doing it? The truth is that this happens all the time. As humans, we have a natural need to be part of a social system, and this need can work for us or against us. It's very difficult to do the right thing when everyone around you is doing the wrong thing. That's why it's important to choose good friends and mentors. **You should never say, do, think, or be anything just because everyone else is doing it.** Your choices in life should be grounded in what you know to be true, and what you feel to be right. Real friends will respect your strength of character.

Obedience

Obedience is a fine line to walk. Especially when you are young. Here is the Merriam Webster Dictionary's definition of what it means to **obey**:

- To follow the commands or guidance of.

- To conform to or comply with.

You can see that "conform" is in the definition for "obey". So, it makes sense that the same principles apply to both concepts. There are many situations where it is in your best interest to obey the authorities in charge – like when your parents or guardians tell you to check in when you get to your friend's house or when you're driving, and a speed limit sign reminds you to slow down for a school zone. Those are the types of rules and commands that you should follow because they are meant to keep you and others safe.

What happens when we start obeying without question? In 1961, a psychologist at Yale University named Dr. Stanley Milgram decided to see how much pain people were willing to inflict on others when instructed to do so by someone with a lot of authority. Subjects were brought into a room with an electroshock machine and told they would be giving a memory test to a person in the next room who was attached to the machine. They were unaware that this person was an actor. During the memory test, whenever the actor pretended to get a question wrong, the subject was instructed to administer an electric shock to the person as a penalty. Of course, it was a fake electric shock – no one was actually getting hurt in this experiment. Each time there was a wrong answer, the shock had to get stronger. **Every single subject** went up to at least 300 volts of electricity before deciding not to do as they were told.[8] For perspective, your standard house plug in the United States carries 120 volts of electricity. That means **every subject** was willing to administer **deadly amounts of electricity** to another person because a scientist was urging them to do so!

I'm not trying to disintegrate your faith in humanity with these examples. I'm trying to demonstrate how easy it is to confuse being part of a supportive group with being part of a mob. I'm trying to tell you that there's nothing wrong with authority unless it is abused. It's good to follow the rules when you understand what function the rules serve. Some rules are there to keep you safe. Some rules are there to help you learn. So, don't act blindly – use your mind(ly). Think about what you're doing and why and help those around you to do the same.

12.3 – Discussion Questions

1. Have you ever been in a real-life situation like the Asch experiment – a situation when everyone around you was thinking or doing something that you knew was wrong? What did you do? Did you go with the group, or did you follow your gut? Why or why not?

2. Have you ever gotten into trouble for "going with the group"? What happened? What would you do differently if you had to do it again?

Chapter 12 References

[1] Camins, S. (2020, September 6). *How to Build a Support System*. Road to Growth Counseling. https://roadtogrowthcounseling.com/how-to-build-a-support-system/.

[2] Feingold, G. (2019, October 24). *The 5 Parts of a Complete Support System*. Coaching with Gabriella. https://gabriellafeingold.com/5-parts-support-system/.

[3] Cherry, K. (2020, April 14). *Social Support Is Imperative for Health and Well-Being*. Verywell Mind. https://www.verywellmind.com/social-support-for-psychological-health-4119970.

[4] Characteristics of Healthy; Unhealthy Relationships. (2018). Retrieved from https://youth.gov/youth-topics/teen-dating-violence/characteristics.

[5] Ohio Department of Education. (2020). Retrieved October 21, 2020, from http://education.ohio.gov/Topics/Other-Resources/News/Help-Teens-KNOW-How-to-Set-Dating-Boundaries.

[6] Asch, S. E., & Guetzkow, H. (1951). Effects of Group Pressure Upon the Modification and Distortion of Judgments. *Organizational Influence Processes*, 295-303.

[7] Asch, S. E. (1956). Studies of Independence and Conformity: I. A Minority of One Against a Unanimous Majority. *Psychological Monographs: General and Applied*, 70(9), 1.

[8] Milgram, S. (1963). Behavioral Study of Obedience. *The Journal of Abnormal and Social Psychology*, 67(4), 371–378. https://doi.org/10.1037/h0040525.

Chapter 13
PERSONALITY

13.1 – Personality 101

Hi y'all, it's Dr. OH here again to talk about personalities. In psychology, **personality** is described as the way we tend to **feel**, **think**, and **behave** in different situations and over time. Understanding the fundamental parts of a person's personality allows you to better communicate with and therefore better understand that person. Because of that, an entire field of psychology has been dedicated to the study of personality.

Why study personality?

Have you ever looked for a job? What do you remember about the job descriptions? Here's a line taken from an actual job posting for a Sales Consultant:

> **"We seek a charismatic, results-oriented, self-motivated candidate with a proven track record of success."**

Charismatic, **results-oriented**, and **self-motivated** are all personality traits. Knowing the type of personality that will be the most successful in a particular job is good for everyone involved.

Take myself as an example. I do not have a hugely social personality, so a job that requires lots of socialization (something like customer service, for example) wouldn't be a good fit for me. But I love research, learning, and teaching so the academic world is a great fit for my personality.

There are well-researched tests for assessing personality, and many companies use these tests when they are looking to hire new employees. Using these tests can help both the employer and the employee be successful.

Knowing how to assess personality also helps us understand personality disorders. These kinds of disorders can be debilitating and sometimes even dangerous for the person with the disorder as well as for those around them. Being able to recognize and understand the details of these disorders is critical to helping those that suffer from them.

And the last reason for studying personality is…drum roll pleeease… it's fun! Who doesn't love a good personality quiz? Now, be aware that most of the quizzes you get from social media or BuzzFeed are not really considered "real" personality tests, so don't bet your career on results from a 1-minute-wonder-quiz. But some of those quizzes capture concepts about personality that are rooted in real science. So, how does real science measure personality?

Measuring your personality

What one word describes your personality the best? Having a hard time coming up with just one word? Good. That's how it should be.

Simply put, personality is not simply put. The way you behave, think, and feel cannot be encompassed by a single term. Personality is not black and white. Historical approaches have considered personality to be influenced by things like:

- **Introversion & Extraversion:** Carl Jung suggested that people can be described by how they are mentally energized. Introverts thrive spending time on their own, while extraverts thrive around other people. Traditionally, you were either introverted or extraverted, but modern theories have evolved to understand that everyone is some combination of the two.

- **Nature vs. Nurture:** This is a centuries-old debate centering on how much of your personality is genetically "built-in", and how much is molded by your environment and upbringing. Most scientists today agree that there is no set answer to this question. Nature and nurture are delicately interwoven, and everyone is dealing with their own, special combination of the two.

- **Birth Order:** Alfred Adler proposed that some part of your personality is determined by your birth order (are you a first or second born? An only child?).

- **Observing Others:** Albert Bandura theorized that you learn aspects of your personality by observing other people.

New approaches use adjectives called **traits** to describe personality. The most popular current theory is called the **Big Five Theory**. The "Big Five" refers to the five trait categories: **Openness**, **Conscientiousness**, **Extraversion**,

Agreeableness, and **Neuroticism**.[1] Put the first letters together for an easy-to-remember anagram: **OCEAN!**

Each category of OCEAN has sets of opposing tendencies or traits, and you have to analyze how you would think, feel, and behave in typical situations. Are you more this way, or more that way? Your Big Five is a snapshot of your personality. That snapshot can change slightly depending on the situation you're in – your personality around your parents might be a bit different from your personality around your friends.

If you want to take an **unofficial just-for-fun test**, you can go through each column below and plot yourself on the little line for each category. Don't overthink it! There are no right or wrong answers here.

Traits	Dimensions		
		Are you more…	
Openness	practical	●——┼——┼——┼——┼——●	imaginative
	conforming	●——┼——┼——┼——┼——●	independent
	routine	●——┼——┼——┼——┼——●	variety-seeking
Conscientiousness	disorganized	●——┼——┼——┼——┼——●	organized
	careless	●——┼——┼——┼——┼——●	careful
	impulsive	●——┼——┼——┼——┼——●	disciplined
Extraversion	retiring	●——┼——┼——┼——┼——●	sociable
	somber	●——┼——┼——┼——┼——●	fun-loving
	reserved	●——┼——┼——┼——┼——●	energetic
Agreeableness	ruthless	●——┼——┼——┼——┼——●	softhearted
	suspicious	●——┼——┼——┼——┼——●	trusting
	uncooperative	●——┼——┼——┼——┼——●	helpful
Neuroticism	calm	●——┼——┼——┼——┼——●	anxious
	secure	●——┼——┼——┼——┼——●	insecure
	self-satisfied	●——┼——┼——┼——┼——●	self-pitying

The Big Five – Your Snapshot

For more information about the Big Five perspective, check out Psychology Today's great overview at https://www.psychologytoday.com/us/basics/big-5-

personality-traits.[2] For another cool just-for-fun test, The Open-Source Psychometrics Project hosts an online questionnaire aimed at gauging your Big Five traits: https://openpsychometrics.org/tests/IPIP-BFFM/.[3]

Remember: It's basically impossible not to influence the outcome of your own personality test. Sometimes we end up picking the traits we prefer (the ones we see as strengths), rather than who we really are. Try not to make that mistake.

Being honest with yourself and discovering the different dimensions of your own personality can help you to put yourself in situations where you will be the most successful. Whether that's a career choice, relationship decision, or the paint color you choose for your bedroom. Your personality is you. Get to know yourself!

13.1 – Discussion Questions

1. What does your personality snapshot look like right now? What will it look like when you're done with class and hanging out with your friends? What will it look like at home?

2. Based on your answer above, how much does your personality change from one situation to the next? Why do you think that is?

3. Is there any part of your personality that you want to have more confidence in?

4. Is there any part of your personality that gets you in trouble from time to time? What can you do to work on that?

13.2 – Nature *and* Nurture

Some traits you're born with: your eye color, hair color, and your height, for example. Your physical traits and many parts of your personality come from your **genes** (genetics), which are part of your **DNA** (deoxyribonucleic acid). Your DNA carries all the information you inherited from your parents. And even though you *can* change your physical appearance, and even though your personality can change a little over time, you cannot change your DNA. Interestingly, **99.9% of every person's DNA is identical.**[4] It's true! Only **0.1%** makes us unique from other humans. That 0.1% determines how you look, how your body functions, your risk for disease, and a lot more. But when it comes to who you are as a person, your genes are only part of the equation. Your environment also plays a huge role in shaping your life.[5]

Your Environment Impacts Your Identity

From the day you were born, you've been taking in all types of information from the environment around you. As a baby, you learned from your parents what safety and love felt like, what foods you liked and disliked, and how to communicate your wants and needs. As a toddler, you probably learned how to argue from your siblings or friends.

As a teenager, you're learning many things from everyone around you: the value of teamwork on the sports field, the reward for hard work in the classroom, and what qualities you like in a friend, for example. People like to say that you become the average of the five people you hang around the most, and there's a lot of truth in that.

It's a good idea to ask yourself this question: ***Am I hanging around the kind of people I want to become?*** These people and your shared experiences with them will shape the person you become. Sure, a lot of your identity is born in you through **nature (genes and DNA)**, but the rest of it – the part you can actually do something about – is formed through **nurture (life experiences)**. The people you hang out with will make a lasting impact on who you become.

Similarities and Differences

As human beings, we have **WAY MORE** similarities than differences. The simple fact that we're human gives us the same baseline. We have the same basic needs. We all need food, shelter, safety, and belonging. We all want to lead a happy life.

So, if that's true, why do so many people focus on what's different? It's human nature. The brain is designed to protect you from anything new, scary and uncertain. If your brain senses that you could be in danger, it sends a signal to your body that says, "Hold up… this isn't safe." For example, when a dog starts chasing you, what do you do? You run away as fast as you can! What happens when you accidentally place your hand on a hot stove? You move it away. While these are actions you don't think about, your brain is always working hard behind the scenes to keep you out of harm's way.

Unfortunately, there are times when your brain works against you. Did you know that when you meet someone for the first time, you're automatically analyzing that person before one word is even spoken? It's automatic.

In a matter of seconds, your brain is taking in a ton of information: facial features, body language, and many more biological cues. And you don't even realize you're doing it! Don't think of this as intentionally being judgmental, it's simply how your brain is wired. First impressions happen in a millisecond![6]

Focus on Similarities

If we don't acknowledge our automatic analyzing, it can quickly lead into judging. So, if you see someone who seems different and start comparing yourself or making a snap judgement, stop and change your thinking to focus on your similarities. What do you have in common? I guarantee it's more than you think.

Replace Judgement with Acceptance.

Judgment happens when we compare ourselves to other people and then jump to conclusions believing that we are somehow better than them.

- "He's so dumb because he failed the test."

- "She's only happy because she's pretty."

- "He's boring because he doesn't talk that much."

Can you feel the **judgement** of those three statements? They don't even make sense! A lot of smart people fail tests. Being attractive doesn't mean your life is easy. Some people are shy in group settings, but with their friends they're the life of the party and you can't get them to shut up.

Put yourself in the other person's shoes.

- How would you feel if you failed the test? There are probably a few times you forgot to study and didn't score as high as you wanted, right?

- What if you're beautiful, but insecure? What if you looked in the mirror every morning and focused on what was wrong and imperfect?

The point is: you never know what's going on in someone's life, so it's a mistake to label or judge anyone. By thinking about what they might be going through in life, you can start to have more empathy and understanding. Our differences shouldn't divide us – they should unite us!

13.2 – Discussion Questions

1. Do you think people are shaped more by nature or nurture? (Just an opinion.)

2. Think about the last time you had a judgmental thought. What was it? How can you change it to acceptance or tolerance for our differences? (You don't have to name names, but it's important to be honest with yourself).

3. What are some ways you can challenge yourself to step out of your comfort zone and connect with someone who may seem different than you?

13.3 – Attachment Styles Shape Your Identity

What's up, guys? Dr. Kirleen here to talk about your "backstory," meaning your past, and how it affects your "today story," meaning who you are today. We all have positive and negative events in our past, especially in our closest relationships, and we need to acknowledge how these events and these people impact who we are today: our self-esteem, identity, behavior, and even our mental health. If you think about it, the most significant relationships you had as a baby and as a young child were with your parents or guardians… or whoever was raising you. They fed you, changed your diapers, and literally kept you alive. Let's focus on those early years of life and your relationships with your adult caretakers.

Sometimes you'll hear people use the term "daddy issues" to describe a woman or a girl who had a poor relationship with her father. It's often used as an insult: "That girl has daddy issues!" While it's easy to see what people mean, I want you to know the term "daddy issues" is a cliché. It holds no real meaning in the world of psychology. It's also incorrectly seen in a female context, but in reality: anyone can be affected.[7]

Even though it's not an official diagnosis, there is some truth behind the idea of "daddy issues." For example, if someone grows up in a chaotic or non-supportive family system, they might feel like they're "never good enough." Over the years, if the person believes that lie, it can lead to many negative outcomes, especially in how that person forms relationships.

Attachment Styles

In psychology, we use the term "attachment style" to describe how these important relationships are formed, especially early in life. Attachment is a deep and enduring emotional bond that connects you to other people.[8] You learn your attachment style at a young age as you bond and attach to your parents or caregivers, and that makes a huge impact on how you "attach" and create meaningful relationships in your life today. Attachment styles are often grouped into the following categories.

1. Secure Attachment

Having a secure attachment style comes from growing up in a household where you have a reliable, dependable relationship with your mother, father, or caregivers. The relationship is reciprocated, meaning they show you love and affection, and you show it back. Children who grow up with secure attachment tend to be happier, kinder, and they have better relationships with their parents, siblings, and friends.[9]

2. Anxious Attachment

Anxious attachment comes from growing up in an unpredictable environment. This can occur if your parents or caregivers had unpredictable mood swings, actions, or behaviors. It makes your life like a rollercoaster. This can lead to anxiety and "walking on egg-shells" as a child. People who grew up with anxious attachment can find themselves being clingy or needy in relationships.

3. Avoidant Attachment

Avoidant attachment comes from growing up in a home where your thoughts and emotions are dismissed or brushed off. If your parents or caregivers were dismissive of you, it could lead to an avoidant attachment style that causes you to dismiss your thoughts and emotions and others' thoughts or emotions. If you grew up with an avoidant attachment style, you may subconsciously try to be emotionally distant or independent from the people you love.

4. Disorganized Attachment

Disorganized attachment usually refers to abuse. It comes from growing up in an environment where you were verbally, mentally, physically, or sexually abused by your parents or caregivers. Disorganized attachment encompasses some of the same outcomes as the anxious and avoidant attachment styles, depending on the situation, but it is usually much more severe. People with a disorganized attachment style may be afraid to get too close to people, but they're also fearful of distancing themselves. They are generally overwhelmed with their reactions to triggers or issues that arise in their relationship, and they often have unpredictable mood swings and outbursts.

Look at The Big Picture

The most important thing to remember about your attachment style is that it's a piece of your childhood that you had no control over. We don't choose our attachment styles, and in many cases, our attachment styles helped us survive and adapt as a child.

The good news is you can change your attachment style as an adult. We all come to the table with something. No one is perfect. But what we speak on, recognize, and accept, we can change.

Signs of Unhealthy Attachment Style

Whether we realize it or not, we tend to seek out relationships that are similar to those we had with our parents or guardians when we were young. If you had an anxious or avoidant relationship with your father or another parent, you might gravitate towards relationships that repeat the same patterns. Some examples of this can include the following:

- Dating the same type of person over and over again, even though it never works. This happens in romantic relationships, but the same type of thing can happen in friendships.

- Sexual promiscuity or being hypersexual can come from abuse, causing you to feel you have to give your physical body to be loved.

- Entering into emotionally destructive relationships that involve violence, fear, bullying and intimidation.

- Neediness, or requiring constant reassurance from close friends or a significant other.

- Keeping your guard up or being emotionally distant because you don't trust people enough to be yourself.

- Giving more than you're getting. This could mean taking on more than your share of the responsibilities in the relationship to ensure the other person never abandons you.

4 Tips for Healing

If you deal with any unhealthy attachment styles, here are 4 tips to help you heal:

1. First of all, don't shame or judge yourself for it. No one is perfect, and we all have things to work on. There is nothing wrong with you! We're all on a journey.

2. If you've had some major negative experiences with your parents, guardians, or caretakers, don't try to deal with it alone. Talk to your parents or a trusted adult in your life, and ask them to help you get an appointment with a professional counselor or a psychologist.

3. Sometimes it can help to write a letter to the parent or the person who hurt you, but you don't have to give it to them. Putting all your thoughts on paper allows you to express what you need to say without repercussions.

4. Finally, pay attention to your emotions and feelings as much as possible. If you get triggered and find yourself being needy or feeling insecure, you don't have to react in a negative way. Allow yourself to "feel your feelings," and then make a choice to respond in a positive way.[10]

13.3 – Discussion Questions

1. What is an attachment style, and how is it formed?

2. Which attachment style is connected to acting clingy, needy, and controlling?

3. What if someone is emotionally distant, and they can never get close to people… which attachment style might they have?

4. Think about what type of attachment style you have with your parental figures and how it affects you today.

5. Are there any hurtful experiences in your past that you've never really addressed? Who are the trusted adults in your life? Hopefully, they're your parents. Is there anything you need to talk about with them?

   (Remember if you've been through any type of abuse, report it to a school counselor or a police officer right away.)

Chapter 13 References

[1] John, O. P., Donahue, E. M., & Kentle, R. L. (1991). Big Five Inventory. *Journal of Personality and Social Psychology.*

[2] Psychology Today (unknown). Big 5 Personality Traits. https://www.psychologytoday.com/us/basics/big-5-personality-traits.

[3] Open-Source Psychometrics Project (August, 2019). Big Five Personality Test. https://openpsychometrics.org/tests/IPIP-BFFM/.

[4] Genetics vs. Genomics Fact Sheet. (2018, September 7). National Human Genome Research Institute. https://www.genome.gov/about-genomics/fact-sheets/Genetics-vs-Genomics.

[5] Hopwood, C. J., Donnellan, B. M., Blonigen, D. M., Krueger, R. F., McGue, M., Iacono, W. G., & Burt, A. S. (2011, March). Genetic and Environmental Influences on Personality Trait Stability and Growth During the Transition to Adulthood: A Three-Wave Longitudinal Study. Journal of Personality and Social Psychology. https://www.ncbi.nlm.nih.gov/pmc/articles/PMC3058678/.

[6] Willis, J., & Todorov, A. (2006, July). First Impressions: Making Up Your Mind After a 100-Ms Exposure to a Face. Psychological Science. https://journals.sagepub.com/doi/10.1111/j.1467-9280.2006.01750.x.

[7] Moore, J. (2017, December 29). What Are "Daddy Issues" Exactly? https://blogs.psychcentral.com/life-goals/2017/12/what-are-daddy-issues-exactly/.

[8] Ainsworth, M. D. S. (1973). The Development of Infant-Mother Attachment. In B. Cardwell & H. Ricciuti (Eds.), Review of child development research (Vol. 3, pp. 1-94) Chicago: University of Chicago Press.

[9] Divecha, D. Ph.D. (2017). How to Cultivate a Secure Attachment with Your Child. https://greatergood.berkeley.edu/article/item/how_to_cultivate_a_secure_attachment_with_your_child.

[10] Brogaard, B. (2015, March 18). How to Change Your Attachment Style. https://www.psychologytoday.com/us/blog/the-mysteries-love/201503/how-change-your-attachment-style.

Chapter 14

TRAUMA

14.1 – Introduction to Trauma

 Hey y'all! Dr. OH here to take a look at how your brain handles trauma. Remember earlier in the book when we talked about stress? Well, multiply stress by a gazillion and you've got trauma. **Trauma** comes from the Greek word for "wound". Originally, the word trauma referred to physical injuries, like breaking a bone. As the word evolved, it also started being used to describe emotional injuries, like losing a loved one. The word can be used in a few different ways:

- **Trauma can be a physical injury.** A bruise on the skin or a brain injury are examples of physical traumas.

- **Trauma can describe a mental injury.** You can be mentally traumatized after being in a car accident.

- **Trauma can describe an event.** A serious car accident is a traumatic event.

What is a traumatic event?

An event is traumatic when it causes extreme stress and significant harm to your physical health, your mental health, or both. Some types of events are known to be traumatic for almost anyone who experiences them.

Common Causes of Trauma

- Being physically or sexually abused
- Being in or witnessing a serious accident that causes injuries or death
- Being in a war or witnessing war-time events
- Being in or witnessing natural disasters or pandemics

Other situations are only traumatic for some people. For example, I love dogs, so if I were tackled by a large, overly-friendly pup in the park – no biggie. But some folks are terrified of dogs, and if the same thing happened to them, it could be really traumatic.

Post-Traumatic Stress Symptoms

Experiencing a trauma can affect many areas of your life. The most extreme product of experiencing a traumatic event is referred to as **Post-Traumatic Stress Disorder** (or **PTSD**). But you don't have to have PTSD to suffer from trauma. Being bullied – even once – can be traumatic. Losing a loved one to cancer is traumatic. The point is, trauma comes in many different forms, and we should never judge someone by their past trauma. Instead, we should try to show empathy, knowing the person's trauma may have had a very real and lasting effect on their life.

Trauma is a direct result of an extreme stressor, so we react to traumatic situations very much like we react to stress. In fact, the effects of trauma are sometimes referred to as **Post-Traumatic Stress Symptoms** (or **PTSS**). The same five components of health that are involved in the stress response are also affected when we experience PTSS. Let's refresh:

- **Physical**: aches, pain, fatigue
- **Social**: loneliness, isolation, resentment
- **Emotional**: irritability, depression, feeling overwhelmed
- **Behavioral**: changes in eating or sleeping patterns, increase in nervous habits
- **Cognitive**: poor concentration, memory trouble, poor judgment, anxiety

Why do your brain and body respond so harshly to trauma? It's because the brain has a very difficult time processing traumatic events. When you're faced with a big stressor, your brain instructs your body to enter a state of **fight-or-flight**, which helps you decide how to react to the stressor. For example, let's say you're out hiking, and you come across a bear.

Your brain says, *"Danger! A bear!"*

Your body says, *"OMG. What do I do??"*

Your brain usually answers in one of two ways:

"Fight the bear! RAWR!"

OR

"Eek! Run away!"

When you go into fight-or-flight mode, it triggers an immediate emotional and physical response. Your brain mobilizes your body to react effectively by releasing hormones. These hormones wake up the adrenal glands that sit on top of your kidneys. Those glands start pumping out adrenaline, cortisol, and a host of other products that increase your heart rate, breathing rate, and metabolism, so your body has the energy it needs to act. The larger the stressor, the greater the response.

These are huge changes for your body to undertake, and **they are exhausting**. Whether physical or emotional, dealing with trauma can be very draining. In fact, trauma can even affect the physical development of your brain (yikes!). A study in the Journal of Adolescent Health[1] found that when a teenager's brain is repeatedly exposed to high levels of cortisol (from stress and trauma), it can affect two areas of the brain in particular:

- **The prefrontal cortex:** the part of your brain responsible for decision making, reasoning, and impulse control. The prefrontal cortex is in the very front of your brain, right behind your eyebrows and forehead.

- **The hippocampus:** the part of your brain largely devoted to memory, but it also has a hand in learning and emotions. The hippocampus is in the center part of your brain, and it's shaped like a seahorse. Interestingly, the Greek word for seahorse is…wait for it…hippocampus!

The involvement of these areas accounts for some of the symptoms of trauma like irritability, memory trouble, and poor judgement. When you experience a traumatic event, it's important to have a grasp on what happens in the brain. This knowledge can help you understand and interpret your experience of trauma. In the next two sections, Dr. Kirleen is going to address the psychological and emotional side of trauma, and most importantly, she's going to give clear insight on the recovery process.

14.1 – Discussion Questions

1. Can you think of any types of situations that might be traumatic for one person, but not for someone else?

2. What is Post-Traumatic Stress Disorder?

3. What are Post-Traumatic Stress Symptoms?

4. What happens in the brain when we go into fight or flight mode?

5. Which area of the brain handles memory?

6. Which area of the brain is responsible for decision-making?

7. Why do you think our experiences of trauma have such lasting effects?

14.2 Learning from Trauma

 Hey friends, it's Dr. Kirleen here to talk about unspeakable experiences, also known as trauma. Life is full of highs and lows, but sometimes our lows can leave a lasting impact on us. Negative experiences can shape our behaviors and how we see ourselves. Unspeakable experiences or trauma can include sexual or physical abuse, betrayal, loss, or even mental and verbal abuse.

As Dr. OH pointed out, when you live through trauma, it chemically changes your brain's makeup, especially if you experience trauma at a young age. As human beings, we try to protect ourselves from trauma, and we often bury it deep down inside. When we bury trauma, we might not talk about it or even think about it for years. You may go through life assuming you're totally over it, but it can show up in how you think and feel about yourself and how you act.[2]

What is an Unspeakable Experience?

An unspeakable experience is a traumatic event that causes a threat to your safety and potentially places your life or the lives of others at risk. As a result, a person experiences high levels of emotional, psychological, and physical distress that temporarily and/or chronically disrupts their ability to function normally.[3] All trauma is different, and trauma can come in many shapes and sizes. Here's a list of some traumatic experiences teens may face.

- Being the victim of abuse (sexual, physical, or emotional)

- Witnessing a violent act

- Bullying (face-to-face or cyberbullying)

- Loss of a parent or friend

- Local, national, or international tragedies (fires, floods, hurricanes, etc.)

Name Your Experience

The first step to learning from trauma is to name it. Not only is this the first step, but it's also the hardest. If you've buried your unspeakable experience, it starts to feel like no one even cares.

Why even mention it? When we bury trauma, we may not think about it or consider it impactful in our lives, but it still affects us. It's a leak in our boat. Even if you don't think about it, talk about it, or consider it, you know it will show up deep down.

Naming it makes it real and tangible and, therefore, something you can do something about. You can name your unspeakable experience by saying it out loud to yourself in the mirror, telling a trusted friend or adult, or simply writing it down in a journal. Once you've named your trauma, you have shifted control from the experiences having power over you to you having power over the experience. Thinking back through your life and digging up the most challenging parts is neither glamorous nor enjoyable. Still, it's necessary to understand how unspeakable experiences have shaped your life.[4]

The Shame Cycle

Shame involves internalizing an experience into meaning you are bad, flawed, or to blame for it happening. Shame makes you feel like **you are bad** instead of **what happened to you was bad**.

Shame is different from guilt. **Shame** is a destructive feeling of being unworthy, bad, or wrong. **Guilt** is the feeling of being responsible for causing harm. Shame is learned from growing up in an environment where shame was taught, sometimes inadvertently, by parents and other caregivers.

The shame cycle occurs when you've buried an unspeakable event. Soon enough, you start to think you deserved your trauma. You feel unworthy or undeserving and blame yourself for the experiences. Anxiety can be a physical manifestation of the shame associated with the unspeakable event. The next step in the shame cycle is medicating these feelings of anxiety. Then, you feel shame for having these feelings and medicating them, which causes more shame. Then, the cycle repeats.

- **Step One:** Bury the unspeakable event, refusing to speak of it.
- **Step Two:** Start to feel as though the trauma defines you and blame yourself for the trauma.
- **Step Three:** Anxiety kicks in, providing a physical manifestation of the shame around the trauma.
- **Step Four:** Medicate feelings of shame and anxiety (overeating, using anger, or substance abuse).
- **Step Five:** Feel shame and repeat.

If you find yourself stuck in the shame cycle, it may be due to a traumatic event in your past. The best advice is to ask your parents or guardians to help setup an appointment for you with a mental health professional. You don't have to bury the pain or live in the shame cycle. Help is available, but you need to be brave and ask for it.

14.2 – Discussion Questions

1. What are some examples of traumatic events or unspeakable experiences?

2. Do you think you've ever experienced something traumatic? If this question is too personal, you are not required to answer (and if it is, we urge you to speak with a trusted adult, such as a parent or a mental health professional).

3. How is shame different than guilt?

4. What could you do if you found yourself stuck in the shame cycle?

14.3 – Recovering from Trauma

 Trauma is so painful that sometimes the brain can repress the memory, making it very difficult to remember. It's almost like the brain doesn't let you go there. There are several signs of repressed trauma that can show up in everyday behavior patterns.

Signs of Repressed Trauma

Trust Issues – If you have been betrayed by a loved one or family member, trust issues can arise. Those with trauma can find it hard to let anyone in, even if it's someone very close to them. Being super independent and pushing people away can stem from trauma.

Shame and Insecurity – Holding shame around an unspeakable event can cause chronic insecurity. Shame is a self-worth killer that can cause insecurity. Those who are chronically insecure may show it by boasting about themselves or trying to one-up anyone with achievements. On the flip side, chronic insecurity could make you painfully shy and withdrawn from others.

Anxiety – Anxiety goes hand in hand with shame. When you carry shame, you become anxious that others will see you the way you see yourself. This can cause you to self-sabotage or chronically overthink things. Overthinking looks like one thought spiraling into another until you've created an unlikely scenario that makes you feel anxious.

Sexual Promiscuity – Those who have been sexually abused may become sexually active or promiscuous. This means they use their body to receive love and validation, even though it's a false validation.

Giving More Than You're Getting – Placing yourself in situations where you're always the giver or the doer can be a sign of repressed trauma. Remember, shame is a self-worth killer, and when your self-worth is low, you accept subpar treatment from those in your life. If you're always the one doing the work in your relationships, you should reevaluate.

PTSD & Depression – Posttraumatic Stress Disorder and depression are common in people who have experienced trauma. If you find you are reliving the event, avoiding triggers of the event, or have little to no motivation for life, talk to someone you trust about seeking professional help.

6 Tools for Healing from a Traumatic Event

Although you may never "fully heal" from a traumatic event, you can still take steps to learn, recover, and start healing[5]. Below are six tools for your journey.

1. **Accept it was not your fault.** When unspeakable events or trauma show up in life, we tend to blame ourselves, especially if it happened when we were children. I want to tell you right now: it was not your fault. I know what you're thinking – "I don't even know you!" But I know without a shadow of a doubt your trauma was not your fault, especially if it happened when you were young.

2. **Name your experience.** Stand in front of a mirror and name your unspeakable experience. Say it out loud and take your power back. Next, tell yourself how your trauma has affected you.

3. **Feel your feelings.** Repressing your feelings and burying your trauma will only keep you stuck in the shame cycle. Once you've named your experience, take time to understand how it makes you feel. Trauma or unspeakable events are stored in the body. Pay attention to where you physically feel tension or pain and send loving energy to that area. Sitting in uncomfortable feelings or emotions isn't easy. Don't hesitate to reach out to someone you trust or a licensed mental health professional if you feel overwhelmed.

4. **Speak to someone who has earned the right to hear your story.** Telling someone you trust about your unspeakable event is a powerful thing. It allows you a new perspective and the opportunity for help if you need it. Don't carry this burden alone because once you speak it, you have the power to change how it affects you. However, the person you choose has to be someone who has shown you they are trustworthy.

5. **Choose how to interpret your unspeakable event.** You don't have to be a victim of your past hurts. You can choose how you think about your trauma. Changing your thought patterns takes time and effort. We have thousands of thoughts a day, but most of them are repetitive. Think of your train of thought as a well-worn hiking trail. Your thoughts have tumbled through there so often. It's second nature to keep going in the same direction. To change your thoughts, you have to create a new trail. If you catch a negative thought headed towards the old trail, change it into a neutral thought. A neutral thought is a truth that allows space for understanding and acceptance.

6. **Get professional help.** The best way to start recovering from trauma is to ask your parents or another trusted adult to help you get an appointment with a psychologist, psychiatrist, or a licensed counselor.

As you've learned in other sections, I'm a big believer in facing things head-on, even if it's a little uncomfortable. I know this section may be a challenge for some of you, but I also know that you are fierce, resilient, and stronger than you know. Remember that people like me and other trusted adults in your life have your back, and we want to be there to support you.

14.3 – Discussion Questions

1. What are some of the possible signs and symptoms of repressed trauma? How can unspeakable experiences or trauma show up in everyday life?

2. Name one step you can take to thrive through unspeakable experiences.

3. If you or someone you know experienced a traumatic event, who would you go to for help and why?

Chapter 14 References

[1] Carrion, V. G., & Wong, S. S. (2012). Can Traumatic Stress Alter the Brain? Understanding the Implications of Early Trauma on Brain Development and Learning. Journal of Adolescent Health, 51(2), S23-S28. https://shorturl.at/guySX.

[2] Bremner, J. (2006). Traumatic Stress: Effects on the Brain. Retrieved from https://www.ncbi.nlm.nih.gov/pmc/articles/PMC3181836/.

[3] Understanding Child Trauma. (n.d.). October, 2020. From https://www.samhsa.gov/child-trauma/understanding-child-trauma.

[4] Understanding the Ways Children Cope With Threats. (n.d.). Retrieved November, 2020, from https://www.blueknot.org.au/Resources/Information/Understanding-abuse-and-trauma/What-is-childhood-trauma/Childhood-trauma-and-the-brain.

[5] To Heal Trauma, Work with the Body | Psychology Today. (n.d.). 2017. Retrieved from www.psychologytoday.com/us/blog/workings-well-being/201708/heal-trauma-work-the-body.

Chapter 15

BOUNDARIES

15.1 – Setting Boundaries

What's up! It's Dr. Kirleen, here to talk about boundaries! You've probably heard someone talk about setting boundaries, but what does that mean? Don't worry, you won't be building fences for this chapter, but we will be learning how to set emotional, verbal, and physical boundaries with other people in our lives. My first experience with setting a boundary came in my junior year of high school. I got my first car, and with that came a whole lot of people who suddenly wanted to be my friend. One person in particular always insisted that she use my car and gas to go places, and when I pushed back, she would give me a guilt trip. I wasn't sure how to keep the friendship and stand up to her at the same time. One of the trusted adults in my life helped me understand that a true friend would be there, regardless. Needless to say, that friendship ended when I put my foot down, but many more true friends showed up.

There will always be "boundary-pushers," but if you keep in mind that standing up for yourself sets the tone for how you will be treated, it gets a little easier. This section will explore what boundaries are, types of boundaries, and how to set boundaries.

What are Boundaries?

Boundaries are the personal limits you set for what you're **willing to accept** and for **what you want to protect** in life.[1] When you set boundaries, you're establishing what's "in-bounds" and what's "out of bounds" for you. Just like in sports, boundaries establish the rules of fair play. Setting good personal boundaries is critical to forming healthy relationships, building self-esteem, and reducing other mental health conditions like anxiety and depression. Setting boundaries is a massive piece of crafting your identity as a growing person. Boundaries can be either rigid or loose, but finding a balance is essential.

A complete lack of boundaries may indicate that your sense of identity and self-esteem needs work. Being mindful about your emotional wellbeing is the first step in setting boundaries with people and situations in your life. Boundaries help you protect your energy and wellbeing.[2]

Types of Boundaries

Physical boundaries include your need for personal space, your comfort with touch, and your physical needs like eating and sleeping. A violation of your physical boundaries can look like standing too close, inappropriate touching, depriving you of food or water, or even someone looking through your phone or notebook.

Verbal boundaries include your need to voice your concerns, opinions, and thoughts. A violation of a verbal boundary looks like not allowing you to speak or be heard, screaming at you, gossiping about you, or saying negative, derogatory things about your integrity and character.

Emotional boundaries involve separating your feelings from another's feelings. A violation of your emotional boundary looks like preying upon your sense of self-worth, betraying trust, lying about you or to you, and demeaning, judging, or manipulating you.

How Boundaries Work

Since we are all unique, setting healthy boundaries can look different for everyone. The type of boundaries you set depends on the setting and one the person you're dealing with. The boundaries you set with a best friend can be different than the boundaries you set with a family member.

One example of setting a boundary would be declining to go out with friends because you have an insane amount of homework to finish. This protects your time and mental wellbeing. Another example would be asking your friend not to touch your things if you aren't comfortable. Of course, you do this from a place of compassion and respect to protect yourself.

Setting boundaries with a romantic partner is essential in maintaining a healthy relationship. This could look like requesting time alone or setting limits on what you are comfortable with physically. The need for boundaries shows up in almost all aspects of life, so be mindful of what makes you uncomfortable compared to what you're comfortable with.

You can have boundaries with yourself as well. Setting personal boundaries is a great way to strengthen your identity. For example, you may set a personal boundary, never to lie. Personal boundaries create your moral code and enforce which values you find the most important.

Six Steps to Setting Healthy Boundaries

Setting boundaries can be difficult because most of us don't like disappointing, and we tend to want to avoid conflict. At the same time, boundary pushers can be persistent and consistent with their efforts to get us to do what they want. However, remember that **you teach people how to treat you,** so learning this skill is a must.

To set healthy boundaries, you have to evaluate your life and determine if and where boundaries already exist. Then, think about your relationships and day-to-day encounters with others. Is there someone or something causing you stress? Once you've determined where you need to set boundaries, you can start bringing them into focus with the steps below.[3]

1. **Identify how your limits have been crossed.** Was it a physical, emotional, or verbal violation? Write down your thoughts or talk with a counselor or a trusted adult (like one of your parents), so you can mentally process what happened. This helps you see the big picture and stay connected to reality.

2. **Give yourself permission.** Boundary pushers have a knack for making us feel guilty. Do not allow fear, guilt, and self-doubt to take up too much headspace. You might fear the other person's response, but boundaries are a sign of a healthy relationship and self-respect. So, give yourself permission to set boundaries in every aspect of your life.

3. **Start small.** Setting boundaries is a skill, and like with any new skill, assertively communicating your boundaries takes practice. Start with a person you feel will be receptive to your new skill and then build upon your success with more difficult people.

4. **Be direct.** As previously stated, setting boundaries can feel uncomfortable, and you may tend to beat around the bush. Be clear and to the point. If someone asks you to do something you don't want to do, just say no. Don't over-explain why you're saying no.

5. **Follow through.** If you are brave enough to set the boundary, you have to stick with it. Allowing someone to break your boundaries shows them that you were not serious in the first place. When you set a boundary, it's essential to state why the boundary is important to you and (when appropriate) put consequences in place for breaking it.

6. **Seek support.** If you're having a hard time with boundaries, seek support from a trusted friend or adult. Remember the story I told you of how a trusted adult helped me learn to set boundaries in high school.

In short, boundaries are all about figuring out what you want out of the relationships in your life. Setting healthy boundaries is an essential part of maintaining your mental health, and we all need to make healthy boundaries part of our lives.

15.1 – Discussion Questions

1. What are healthy boundaries, and why are they important?

2. What are some examples of verbal, emotional, and physical boundaries?

3. What are some examples of violations of the three types of boundaries?

4. Take out a fresh piece of paper and write a private journal entry. No one has to see it unless you feel the need to share it with them. In your own words, describe a time when someone violated your own personal boundaries or a time when you violated someone else's. Lastly, take time to reflect and answer this question… what is the right thing to do about it?

15.2 – Difficult Personality Types

We all have difficult people in our lives, but when you're dealing with dysfunctional personalities, it can really mess with your thoughts and emotions.[4] Becoming aware of some classic difficult personality types is important when making decisions about who to date and who to be friends with. Below are seven difficult personality types to watch out for.[5]

1. Negative Ned / Negative Nancy. A Negative Ned or Nancy is someone with a consistent negative perspective, regardless of the circumstance. These are people who don't want to hear solutions to their problems, but instead, want to complain. They always find something wrong wherever they go. These people can be very emotionally draining.

2. Bullies. Bullies are in your face about how they feel, what they want, and what they need from you. They can intimidate you physically or emotionally. They find it hard to take no for an answer, and they pressure you to always be doing what they want. If you say no, they try to make you feel guilty. Bullies can be very manipulative.

3. Blamers. Blamers will not take responsibility for their actions. Nothing is ever their fault. They will turn any confrontation around and make it about you. They have a hard time apologizing, and if they do, it rarely sounds sincere. They usually deflect the blame onto someone or something else, or they say it was a total accident. They accept the lie of their own perfectionism, so admitting a mistake is out of the question.

4. Passive Aggressive. Passive aggressive people say yes, even if they want to say no. They have a hard time speaking their mind in fear of judgment. Instead of saying what they mean, they show it through their behavior. For example, you could ask them to watch your dog, and they say yes. But when the time comes, they arrive 45 minutes late. They couldn't bring themselves to tell you that they didn't want to help out, so instead… they showed you. Their words and actions don't match up.

5. Comparison Junkies. Comparison junkies have to one-up you. If you bring up an achievement, they have something bigger and better to bring to the table. They are always comparing and trying to outdo in every aspect. Sometimes these people are simply overcompensating or projecting larger-than-life to make up for their own subconscious insecurities.

6. Narcissists. Narcissists are people who display a pattern of self-centered, arrogant thinking, and behavior. They lack empathy and consideration for other people, and they have an excessive need for admiration.[6] Consider this a huge leak in their boat. Narcissism is a personality disorder that affects all aspects of one's life. True narcissists believe they are special or unique. Under all the bravado, most narcissists struggle with shame and low self-esteem.

7. Borderline Personality Disorder: People with borderline personality disorder view things in extremes, such as everything is perfect, or everything is falling apart. Their opinions of other people can also change quickly. An individual who they are cool with one day may be considered an enemy the next. These shifting feelings lead to intense drama-filled relationships.

At the core, people with borderline personality disorder are usually trying to avoid real or imagined abandonment. So, they can come across as clingy and overbearing one day and distant and cold the next.

Borderline personality is a mental health disorder, and it can only be diagnosed by a doctor or a mental health professional.

15.2 – Discussion Question or Journal Entry

Without naming any specific names, describe a time when you dealt with a difficult personality type (use one of the types listed in this section). Describe how you dealt with this person and how you might deal with them in the future.

15.3 – Anger Management

Anger is a normal emotion, and we've all felt it at some point. But how do you know if you are managing anger in a healthy way? One of my very first jobs as a therapist was helping teens heal from the effects of living with an angry, violent adult. I learned that anger has lasting negative effects. Even when no one "gets hurt" physically, anger can still be very emotionally damaging. Research shows that living in an anger-filled home can cause kids and teens to have less empathy for others and make more destructive decisions with their lives.[7]

As we read this section, I want you to think about how you handle anger, but I also want you to think about how anger is displayed to you. Remember to reach out to your school counselor, your parents, or another trusted adult if you are in a situation where anger is being excessively directed toward you. This section focuses on when anger falls out of the normal range and becomes unhealthy. We will discuss what it means to be angry, how to control it, and how to know if you're expressing your anger in a healthy way.

What is Anger?

Anger is a natural response to perceived threats. It causes your body to release adrenaline, your muscles to tighten, and your heart rate and blood pressure to increase. Anger can range from mild irritation to intense fury and rage. If these things occur long-term, they can lead to health conditions like heart disease and diabetes.[8] I think of anger as a "surface emotion" because typically there are other "deeper" emotions causing the anger.[9]

The way we see anger expressed growing up plays a huge role in how we handle it later on. As a society, we've been taught that anger is bad and that we shouldn't be experiencing it. This is false. Anger is an essential piece of our mental framework. Without it, we wouldn't be able to defend ourselves from a threat. That said, it shouldn't be the only emotion you use to express frustration. When anger is experienced frequently at intense levels, we have a problem. So, what is the middle ground, and how can we express anger in a healthy way?

5 Indicators of Unhealthy Anger

1. **If you're holding it all inside.** If you're continually repressing your anger and "boiling" beneath the surface, you're letting the anger have too much control in your life. Everyone has difficult moments, but if you get in the habit of stewing in your anger, then it's time to reevaluate your anger management tools.

2. **If small things set you off.** If you notice you're always on-edge, or if minor inconveniences make you explode, you should consider how you're handling anger. You should be able to respond to mistakes and minor inconveniences without doing things you regret. Anger is very reactive, so if you frequently get triggered and lash out instead of thinking through the situation's outcome, you're in the problematic zone.

3. **If you're aggressive physically or verbally.** If you're continually belittling the people, you spend time with hurtful words, or if you've been physically aggressive, you're in the problematic zone of anger.

4. **If you blame others for your anger.** It's easy to blame other people for your anger. A trigger usually comes from outside ourselves, so if someone makes you angry, you blame them. This is problematic because you decide to explode, punch the wall, or belittle people. No one makes you do that.

5. **If a close a friend or family member tells you** they think you have anger issues, this should be a huge sign to you. Remember: if you're in the habit of reacting instead of responding, you may block this out. If important people tell you that your anger is too much, take a step back and listen to them.

The Difference Between Rage and Anger

It's normal to feel moments of anger, but it's not normal to feel rage. Maybe someone ate your leftovers in the fridge, and this makes you feel angry for the moment. That's natural. But if you're feeling rage over your leftovers, then it's probably not about the leftovers. Rage builds over time. It sometimes comes from not feeling heard, understood, respected, or included. **Rage is an explosion of emotion that is out of control.** It's loud, violent, scary, and can show up without warning. When rage is in full flow, there is little room for talking the person down or for empathy, understanding, or clarity. People who experience rage say that they just see red and feel a loss of control in the moment. Rage is a powerful force that creates havoc and can result in physical and emotional harm.[10]

In many cases, rage comes from our backstory. When you peel back the layer of rage, you find the real source of the emotions hiding underneath. Emotions like anxiety, depression, loss, or guilt can transform into rage. If someone in your life is using rage as a way to express emotions, it's time to talk to a trusted adult (like your parents or a guardians). I know asking for help can feel overwhelming, but please know adults like your parents, school counselors, and teachers want to be there for you. You just have to give them a chance.

How to Handle Anger

Because anger can hit suddenly and escalate quickly, it's difficult to address it in the moment. However, there are some things you can do ahead of time to manage your anger in the future.

1. **Write it out.** Take time to journal and write out your daily experiences: positive, negative, and neutral. Think about how things made you feel and your reactions to them. You may start to notice a trend. As you reflect on any negative experiences and your responses to them, you can learn to process your emotions and respond in a positive way (meaning… without getting even).

2. **Talk to yourself, a friend, a parent, or another trusted adult.** Get those thoughts out of your head! Whether you're taking a walk, cleaning your room, or doing chores, talk to yourself about what is going on in your head. This is a great way to clarify your thoughts and release built-up tension.

3. **Get your exercise.** We know that anger is a chemical reaction in the brain with physical side effects. If you can release that adrenaline through exercise, you will have better control over your anger.

4. **Listen to your body.** Even if you do everything right, someone or something will trigger you eventually. When this happens, pay attention to how your body feels. Your heartbeat will spike, and your body temperature will rise. When you start feeling these things, stop and take some deep breaths to slow down the part of the brain that causes anger. As you breathe you can "press pause" in your mind and make a more rational decision (instead of an irrational reaction).

5. **Know your anger triggers.** As you practice the four steps above, you'll start to become more aware of your anger triggers. Rehearse those situations that bother you and practice responding in a way that would make you proud. After a while, responding thoughtfully (instead of reacting negatively) will start to feel normal to you. If you keep at it, **you really can learn how to control your anger** – that way it doesn't control you.

15.3 – Discussion Questions

1. What is anger, and how have you seen it displayed most often?

2. What is the difference between anger and rage?

3. Who can you talk to if excessive anger is being directed towards you?

4. Write a journal entry below. The next time you are feeling overwhelmed with anger, what can you do to manage your anger more effectively?

Chapter 15 References

[1] Tartakovsky, Margarita. "10 Way to Build and Preserve Better Boundaries." Psych Central, 8 Oct. 2018. https://psychcentral.com/lib/10-way-to-build-and-preserve-better-boundaries/.

[2] Brenner, A. "7 Tips to Create Healthy Boundaries with Others." Psychology Today, 31 Oct. 2020. https://www.psychologytoday.com/us/blog/in-flux/201511/7-tips-create-healthy-boundaries-others.

[3] The No-BS Guide to Setting Healthy Boundaries. 2020, www.healthline.com/health/mental-health/set-boundaries.

[4] Characteristics of Healthy; Unhealthy Relationships. (2018). Retrieved October 12, 2020, from https://youth.gov/youth-topics/teen-dating-violence/characteristics.

[5] Ryback, R. (2016, November 16). The Five Types of People You Need to Get Out of Your Life. Retrieved from https://www.psychologytoday.com/us/blog/the-truisms-wellness/201611/the-five-types-people-you-need-get-out-your-life.

[6] Narcissism. (n.d.). Retrieved October 12, 2020, from https://www.psychologytoday.com/us/basics/narcissism.

[7] Vassar, G. (2011). How Does A Parent's Anger Impact His or Her Child? Lakeside Educational Network. https://lakesidelink.com/blog/lakeside/how-does-a-parents-anger-impact-his-or-her-child/

[8] Mayo Clinic Staff. Anger Management: Your Questions Answered. Mayo Clinic, 5 March. 2020. From https://www.mayoclinic.org/healthy-lifestyle/adult-health/in-depth/anger-management/art-20048149.

[9] Anger. 2017, www.apa.org/topics/anger.

[10] "Anger." Psychology Today, 2018, www.psychologytoday.com/us/basics/anger.

Chapter 16

DEPRESSION

16.1 – What is Depression?

Hi, it's Dr. Kagan again. I want to talk with you about depression. Do you ever feel negative emotions like sadness, irritability, or hopelessness? Of course, you do! Everyone experiences these emotions from time to time, especially during the teen years. And things can happen like getting a bad grade, getting cut from a sports team, having a conflict with a friend, or having an argument with your parents. These events can stir strong, negative emotions, and if you're just "feeling depressed" your feelings tend to come and go in a matter of days. Life can be a rollercoaster. That's not depression. **Clinical depression**, meaning the diagnosable type, is more complex than that, and it can last for weeks, months or even years.[1]

Before I talk about clinical depression, let me give you my top six ways to reset your mind when your day is feeling wrecked or when you're having more temporary feelings of depression. Sometimes we can snap out of sadness or negative moods, but we need a plan so we can be proactive. Here's my plan:

6 Ways to Reset a Temporary Depressed Mood

1. Stay positive. That doesn't mean to ignore or deny your feelings of sadness or upset. But you can look at the positive aspects of your life. Stay involved in activities you enjoy.

2. Accept and express your feelings about what is bothering you. Share those feelings, thoughts, and the circumstances with a trusted adult whether it's your parents, teachers, counselors, relatives or friends. I know sometimes you think it makes matters worse to talk with an adult, but a trusted adult will be there for you and get you the help you need, if necessary.

3. **Don't isolate yourself.** Isolation can make your negative mood worse. Spend time with your friends. Sometimes you may need to use technology to stay connected. Call or video-chat and use your voice and talk, rather than type.

4. **Practice healthy habits.** That includes regular physical activity, eat right, avoid alcohol and drugs, and get at least 8 hours of sleep.

5. **Learn how to manage emotions, stress, and anxiety.** Your health teachers, physical education teachers, and counselors may be offering wellness education focusing on stress management, meditation and mindfulness, and emotion management. Trust me, it really does help.

6. **Cut back on passive social media.** I know we all love our technology. But sometimes social media can be a negative influence when we feel down, especially when we're passively viewing content, rather than actively talking to others online. Passive media use can sometimes worsen already negative feelings. Keep in mind, the social contact that media offers is not always supportive, genuine, or in our best interest. When it's draining you emotionally, that's when to cut back.

16.1 – Discussion Questions

1. How would you describe the differences between **clinical depression** and **temporary feelings of depression?**

2. What types of negative situations can lead you to feelings of depression in your life? (Even if the feelings are temporary, they still matter.)

3. Explain what you think Dr. Kagan meant by "passive social media" and describe how it can be emotionally draining.

4. Of the **6 Ways to Reset,** which one are you already doing a good job with?

5. Of the **6 Ways to Reset,** which one seems to have the most potential to help you if you were to develop it more in your life?

16.2 – Clinical Depression

Hey friends, Dr. Kagan here. As a psychologist, I've worked with many teens who have experienced depression (both temporary feelings and longer lasting, clinical depression). When negative, down feelings last a while and are not due to an adverse event or single situation in your life, you may have depression.[2] I want to say this right at the onset: if you find you are depressed, it's not the end of the world. **Depression is the most common mental health condition in the United States.** During the COVID pandemic, everyone and every family faced many difficult challenges. Depression was at an all-time high![3] The good news is: there are things you can do to manage depression. You have the capacity to get better, and there are people who can help.

First, I have a questionnaire on depression for you. Answer these questions honestly and openly. It will give you an understanding of your emotions, which is most important in helping you feel better.

Depression Questionnaire (circle your answers below)

- Do you feel a lack of energy, down in the dumps for no reason or filled with negative emotions like anger, irritability, and sadness? (YES | NO)
- Do you find yourself withdrawing from friends or family? (YES | NO)
- Are you not able to concentrate? (YES | NO)
- Are you defiant and having arguments with everyone? (YES | NO)
- Are you going to the school nurse or your private doctor a lot and they can't find anything wrong with you? (YES | NO)
- Are you experiencing significant weight loss or weight gain? (YES | NO)
- Do you have thoughts or talk about death and suicide? (YES | NO)

- Do you engage in risky or self-destructive behavior like taking drugs, drinking alcohol, or cutting? (YES | NO)

- Do you feel overwhelmed? (YES | NO)

- Do you find you can't pinpoint specific reasons why you feel sad and depressed? (YES | NO)

If you answered yes to many of these questions, you may be experiencing depression. Notice I said, "you may be experiencing depression". It's not for you, your friends or your family to diagnose depression. That's the professional's job. Depression is long lasting, lingering for weeks, months or even longer. It can affect your ability to function normally. Remember, a key message in this book is that it's nothing to be ashamed about. We all have difficult emotional times. Let's honor our feelings and work with them. We can help ourselves and get professional help if we need it. More on that later.

Depression usually isn't caused by a single reason or situation. It may be triggered by a number of events.[4] Some of the common triggers of depression include:

- The death of a loved one

- Parents separating or getting a divorce

- Stress at home

- Moving to a new home

- Stress related to school, like poor grades, bullying or adjusting to a new school

- Serious illness or injury

- Ongoing difficulties of any kind (even if they seem insignificant to others)

Professionals who help people with depression also note that brain chemicals, hormones, and genetics can also play a role in depression. That's why a mental health or medical professional may recommend both a medical evaluation, which involves seeing your doctor, and psychological support, consisting of seeing a counselor or therapist for counseling. We do know that when depressed, we can sometimes make unhealthy life choices and, for example, use alcohol or drugs to cope. Often, that can result in deeper depression and a greater challenge to getting the help we need. So be wise and avoid unhealthy activities. Thoughts of self-harm and suicide may also occur, and we must be aware of those negative thoughts to alert us that we need immediate help.

Keep in mind there are more serious forms of depression when you can't snap out of depression on your own. You realize you are unable to enjoy life and be productive, and you have thoughts of self-harm. It's not a sign of weakness to ask for additional professional help when you are struggling with depression. It is such a relief when you can speak to someone who cares and will help you. It takes courage and strength to take that step of asking for help. You can do it. I promise you it will be one of the best decisions you make. In school, mental health professionals can provide emotional support and help you learn coping skills. You may also seek out private professional support outside of school. Depression can be successfully treated – with psychotherapy, and medical treatment, if necessary. Again, the good news is, help is available. The most serious forms of depression which are categorized as mood disorders need specialized treatment and will be discussed in a future chapter.

Let's also see how our understanding of depression fits with the boat metaphor. Depressive thoughts as any feelings or emotions are like a compass in sailing. Compasses offer us feedback, so we can make navigation corrections. Being aware of our depression allows us to make corrections in how we live our lives.

Back during the pandemic, I recognized that I felt depressed and sad due to all the social isolation. By being aware of my emotions I started reaching out more, contacting my family and friends on the telephone, FaceTime and Zoom (active social media). This greatly provided me some relief and I felt less depressed. I know you can do the same.

Don't avoid, ignore, or be embarrassed by depressive thoughts. Accept them so you can become aware what is bothering you and like a "compass" when sailing, it will help you journey through rough waters, and make positive, healthy choices. Remember: if you are experiencing significant depression, let your parents or a helpful adult in your life know, reach out to a counselor at school, or seek professional psychological help outside of school.

16.2 – Discussion Questions

1. If you answered "yes" to most of the items in the Depression Questionnaire, is there someone in your support system you can talk to about it? What do you think should be your next steps?

2. Now that you have a better understanding of depression, what are some healthy steps for managing depression in everyday life?

3. Which parts of the boat metaphor can be used as tools for managing depression in a more positive way?

4. Which parts of the boat metaphor could contribute to feelings of depression?

5. If you suspected a friend of yours was clinically depressed, meaning depressed for more than a week or two, what could you do to help your friend?

16.3 – Personal Reflection Journal

- Take a few minutes to journal about a time (or times) in your life when you had temporary feelings of depression or when you were depressed for a longer period of time. Use the following writing prompts to get started: **What circumstances may have contributed to your feelings of depression? What was going on in your life at the time? What did you do to feel better and help improve your depression?**

- Write down your key takeaway from that experience. Were there any positive (or negative) things that came out of a depressive episode or time in your life? (For example, I learned from my experience with depression that I could be resilient and bounce back from a difficult time.)

Chapter 16 References

[1] Teen Depression, National Institute of Mental Health, 2020.
https://www.nimh.nih.gov/health/publications/teen-depression/index.shtml.

[2] Depression, KidsHealth.org, Reviewed by D'Arcy Lyness, Ph.D., August 2016.
https://kidshealth.org/en/teens/depression.html.

[3] Rogers, A. A. (2020, September). Teens' Experiences in the Age of COVID-19. Psychology Today. https://www.psychologytoday.com/us/blog/thriving-teens/202009/teens-experiences-in-the-age-covid-19.

[4] Information on Risk Behaviors for Parents with Teens, Centers for Disease Control and Prevention, September 2019. https://www.cdc.gov/parents/teens/risk_behaviors.html.

Chapter 17

ANXIETY

17.1 – What is Anxiety?

Hi y'all, it's Dr. OH again. Remember when we talked about mental illness earlier in the book? We said that *everyone* experiences periods of time when they are mentally unwell, just like everyone experiences being physically unwell. Let's focus here on one of the mental "speedbumps" that we mentioned in that discussion – anxiety.

Anxiety is kind of like nervousness, but it doesn't go away when it's supposed to. Everyone gets nervous about different things. It's nature's way of making sure we stay alive. When people, animals, places, or situations make us nervous, we are more careful around them and that's a good thing. But if your nervousness lasts for a really long time and starts causing more physical and mental distress, you might be suffering from anxiety.

According to the American Psychological Association **anxiety** is "an emotion characterized by feelings of tension, worried thoughts and physical changes like increased blood pressure."[1] Notice the word *emotion* in that definition. Ever heard of an emotion that wasn't natural? Me neither. We all have emotions. They are the result of the neurotransmitters we discussed in the Brain Basics section. For example, the neurotransmitter serotonin is associated with happiness (and a bunch of other things). Anxiety is part of being human.

The most important thing to remember about your anxiety is this: with the right treatment approach, anxiety is one of the factors in your life that *you can control*. In fact, we talk about two excellent approaches for managing anxiety right here in this book: Cognitive-Behavioral Therapy, or CBT, and biofeedback. How do I know they are excellent? Research! A study recently compared 27 different kinds of anxiety treatment approaches and found Cognitive-Behavioral Therapy to be the most successful treatment option.[2]

How else do I know that CBT and biofeedback are great tools? Because I use them myself. I've dealt with anxiety and depression since I was about 12 years old. Before I got proper treatment, I was not only suffering mentally, but also physically. I put all of my worries in my stomach and was sick for a long time (we're talking years). When I was in my 20s, I had some biofeedback therapy to help with my anxiety. The techniques I learned have since gotten me through tons of uncomfortable moments. Combined with therapy and medication, my mental health is well under my control.

How do I know if I have anxiety?

When you're anxious about something, you often can't stop yourself from thinking about that something. Even when you make a real effort not to think about it, the worrying thoughts keep popping up to nag at you. You might experience problems falling asleep because your mind keeps "buzzing". You might have headaches or stomach problems. Maybe you avoid being social when you're anxious about something, or maybe you cling extra tight to family and friends. You might find yourself eating more or less as a way to cope with the stress of constant worrying. For me, it's pie. Or cake. BRB, need cake.

Wading through these kinds of problems is all part of the normal experience of anxiety. But as with many things in life, too much of certain emotions is not a good thing. When you experience too much anger, fear, sadness, or anxiety it can become a disorder. We aren't talking about disorders in this section – you'll hear more about that later from Tom. But by putting anxiety in the context of other normal emotions, I am hoping that you will realize how much control you have over your experience of anxiety. Having control means that, with the proper information and support, you can handle it if and when it becomes a problem.

17.1 – Write a Journal Entry

1. Based on what you've learned about anxiety, do you think you have ever experienced anxiety? What symptoms did you experience?

2. If you experience anxiety often, what do you do to manage it?

3. What could you do to be helpful if you were experiencing high anxiety?

4. How could you help a friend who was feeling a lot of anxiety?

17.2 – Anxiety is not one-size-fits-all

I want to emphasize that, just like *every* other aspect of mental health, anxiety presents differently for different people. The disruptions to life routines can be equally as severe, and the physical expressions can be similar (increased blood pressure, heart rate, sweating, nausea, headaches, etc.) but your experience of anxiety is personal. That doesn't mean that you can't relate to others, or that others can't relate to you.

Are there different kinds of anxiety?

Yes. It is totally possible to have anxiety about one situation and not others. Some people suffer from test anxiety, so they might have symptoms of anxiety for a few days before an exam. Others have social anxiety, which means they get anxious when they have to interact with lots of people, sometimes even if those people are friends. Public speaking and/or performing in front of others (playing music or sports, for example) are also activities that can give folks a lot of anxiety.

Everyone is different, which means that everyone experiences life differently. What makes one person anxious, might not do the same for someone else. However, most – if not all – people will agree that anxiety is really unpleasant. So be kind if you know someone is experiencing anxiety. Knowing how it feels for you puts you in a better position to be empathetic, compassionate, and supportive of that person.

You are not alone.

Please believe me when I tell you that others like you have suffered and then **_conquered_** their anxiety. The New York Times has a wonderful piece that is a collection of letters sent in by teens who have struggled with anxiety for different reasons. You can find the link at the end of this chapter.[3] Here are a couple of quotes from the article to give you a feel for the content:

"It was crippling, the way I viewed the world. I was stuck with this feeling that nothing I was doing was good enough and that I'd never live up to his standards."

"I rarely left my room, afraid that if I didn't stay in studying I would fail all of my exams and never go to medical school."

All of the stories in the article end with a point of "profound resilience and insight". Tom and Dr. Kirleen will talk to you about resilience later in the book, so for our purposes I'll just say that these stories are an excellent demonstration of self-reflection, self-respect, and strength in the face of this very real mental health struggle. Give them a read and get inspired!

Don't be afraid of your anxiety – learn about it so that you can be proactive in getting rid of it. You already have more control than you think, and knowledge is extra power!

17.2 – Discussion Questions

1. Grab a piece of paper and write down a situation that makes you feel anxious or has made you anxious in the past – don't put your name on it. Fold up your paper, and give it to your teacher or group leader.

2. Grab another piece of paper. As your teacher or group leader reads each situation aloud, write down how anxious you would be in that situation on a scale of 1 to 5, with 1 being the least anxious and 5 being the most.

3. Compare your lists of numbers with other students. Do your numbers all match? What does this tell you about how people experience anxiety?

17.3 – Rational vs. Irrational Fear

Hey everybody, it's Tom again. As Dr. OH explained, anxiety is a part of life for everyone, and it does have a purpose. A small amount of anxiety is normal because it helps us navigate around dangerous situations. Anxiety disorders occur when the brain and body see a normal situation and interpret it as dangerous. This triggers our flight or fight response and raises stress hormones in the body.[4]

Many people struggle with anxiety because they have trouble seeing the difference between rational (logical) fears and irrational (illogical fears). The teenage brain finds it especially difficult because the prefrontal cortex (the part governs that rational thought) is one of the last areas to fully develop.

Rational Fear

Rational fear is being afraid of something that can actually hurt you. For example, if you're in a car traveling fast down the freeway in heavy traffic with bad weather, you may be afraid of getting in a car wreck. That fear is rational and logical. It helps you use caution when needed. Or perhaps your friends are about to jump off of a cliff into deep water, and something inside tells you not to do it. That is also rational. If you are faced with a potentially dangerous situation and fear arises, your brain and body are doing their job of keeping you safe.

Not all rational fears have to be dangerous. Some rational fears can come from your academic or personal life. For example, you may be afraid of failing a test that determines your final grade. You could also be afraid of losing an older family member, especially if they have a health condition. These fears are to be expected and worked-through. They are logical fears, based on rational thoughts.[5]

Irrational Fears

Even if the fear is irrational (meaning not logical), it still feels real to the person experiencing it at the time. This creates a fine line between rational and irrational fear. **Irrational fear happens when you're afraid of something that isn't likely to happen.** For example, I have an irrational fear that I'm kind of embarrassed to tell you about. But whatever… I'll tell you. I'm afraid of metal chain-link basketball hoop nets. I can't dunk a basketball or anything like that, but I'm afraid that if I jump up there and swat the net with my hand, then one of my fingers will get caught, and plop! I'll become a finger donor. (I can't believe I just told you that.) But anyway, why is that an irrational fear? It's irrational because I only know of one of those nets in my entire city, and if I go to that specific park, no one is going to force me to jump up there like a buffoon and loose a finger!

Except my son, Jack. He'll make me do it. So, there we were, shooting hoops when this other kid comes over, and we let him join in. Of course, the kid asks if I can dunk, and my son starts laughing (I'm only 5' 9"). The kid asks why Jack is laughing, so Jack tells him all about my irrational fear of the metal nets. Then of course, they beg me to jump up and hit the net. (Fine. I'll do it.) So I jump up there and smack it good. And would you believe it? I actually survived with all of my fingers. I'm a hero.

I turned around and asked the kid what was his greatest fear. He said it was sharks. (Seems rational enough.) But then again, we were living in Michigan at the time, which is nowhere near an ocean! So I asked how many times he'd been to the ocean. He said he'd never been there, but he was afraid of swimming in Lake Michigan (which is freshwater… meaning no sharks). My son and I smiled, and I said to the kid, **"Ya know what? You're gonna fit right in!"** We laughed, and I explained about the sharks and gave him my speech about rational and irrational fear. (Gotta face those irrational fears!) Anxiety is like that sometimes. It finds a way to creep in, even when it doesn't make sense, even when there is no danger to speak of, we somehow let it have power over us. We let it hold us back.

Managing Fear & Anxiety

It can sometimes be difficult to see the difference between rational and irrational fears. Regardless of which category we're looking at, your fear is valid. Both types of fear have the same effect on the body. We are all afraid of something, but the problem arises when fear prevents us from living a normal life.

If you're living with ongoing anxiety, for any reason, talk with your parents, guardians, or with a mental health worker. Anxiety is one of the most common mental health issues, and you are not alone. Working with your doctor or therapist, you can discover the kind of treatment or medicine that works for you.

17.3 – Discussion Questions

1. Do you have any irrational fears that you're willing to share with the group?

2. Can you think of any fears that would be rational for some people, but irrational for others?

3. Who can give an example of someone who made a choice to face their fear? It could be something from your own life or from someone else.

4. If you were with someone and they started breathing heavily and having an **anxiety attack** or a **panic attack**, what would you do to help them?

5. **NOTE:** In Mental Health First Aid, we teach that you should ask the person if they think they're having a panic attack. If they can't give a clear answer, assume they're having a **mental health crisis** and call 911 right away. We are not medical professionals, so we cannot tell the difference between a panic attack, a heart attack, or even an asthma attack. If there's any doubt, call 911. Help the person find a place to sit, offer a glass of water, and wait with them.

Chapter 17 References

[1] American Psychological Society. (2020). Anxiety. Retrieved from https://www.apa.org/topics/anxiety.

[2] Schwartz, C., Barican, J. L., Yung, D., Zheng, Y., & Waddell, C. (2019). Six decades of preventing and treating childhood anxiety disorders: a systematic review and meta-analysis to inform policy and practice. Evidence-based mental health, 22(3), 103-110.

[3] Yin, A. (2017). Coping With Teenage Anxiety: Readers Share Their Stories. New York Times. Retrieved from https://www.nytimes.com/2017/10/23/magazine/coping-with-teenage-anxiety-readers-share-their-stories.html.

[4] National Council for Behavioral Health. (2016). Mental Health First Aid USA: For Adults Assisting Young People. Washington DC: National Council for Behavioral Health.

[5] Walden, A. (2020, January 21). Difference Between Rational vs. Irrational Fear and Its Effects. Health Research Policy. https://www.healthresearchpolicy.org/rational-vs-irrational-fear/.

Chapter 18

COPING SKILLS

18.1 – Take Time to Reset

Hey everybody, it's Tom again. Back when the COVID-19 pandemic sent the world into lockdown, all of my school assembly speeches cancelled for the year, and that's when another crisis dawned on me. I was not thinking about the **healthcare crisis** or the **economic crisis**. Instead… I was thinking about the coming **mental health crisis** and what I could do about it. Immediately I applied to become a certified trainer in **Mental Health First Aid**. Soon, I was accepted, trained, and certified to teach their eight-hour course. Still, I knew many schools didn't have the time or the budget for an all-day mental health training.

The only in-person speech that **wasn't** cancelled for me due to pandemic was at Starbucks Corporate Headquarters in Seattle. It was a video speech we filmed in front of an audience of about 10 people, and they made the video available to all their employees (around the world!). The topic was: **How to be Resilient in the Face of Bullying and Harassment**. Our goal was to give the Starbucks employees the tools to cope with the stress and handle each situation with dignity. Every person I met on that trip talked about the mental stress of the pandemic. And even today, post pandemic, we still live in a very stressful and anxious world.

While the pandemic caused stress for me and my family, it also gave me a renewed drive to create more mental health lessons that teachers could use in schools. I started collaborating with a team of likeminded people in three different states (including Dr. OH and Dr. Kirleen, by the way). Together, we formed a brand-new nonprofit called Reset Schools at https://ResetSchools.org. Our goal is to partner with schools to teach positive coping skills for stress and anxiety. We believe everyone deserves a chance to reset!

What are Coping Skills?

Coping skills are how we deal with the stress and anxiety of life. If we're proactive and choose healthy coping skills, we can handle our stress in a positive way.[1] And on the flip side, if we merely react to stress, our default coping mechanisms can often lead us in the wrong direction, such as overeating, drinking, yelling at our loved ones, blaming others, and all kinds of destructive decisions. In the boat metaphor, ineffective coping is characterized by the leak in the boat. All that overeating only makes the leak bigger, so the boat takes on more water. Get it? That's why it's important to choose healthy coping skills – they stop the leak, fill your tank, and get your engine running again.[2] Now you're going places.

As we formed our nonprofit, Reset Schools, we discovered two distinct categories of what we call "**reset skills**," meaning activities that are proven to reduce stress and improve mental focus. Granted, there are many subcategories, but we call the big two **Calming** and **Boosting** because they help us understand what we want to achieve. **Calming Resets** activate the vagus nerve and the parasympathetic nervous system, creating an immediate calming effect in our brains and bodies.[3] **Boosting Resets** awaken the senses by releasing endorphins and dopamine, giving us a mental boost and renewed focus to face the next challenge. Like any skill, they require time and practice before you see any significant results.[4]

Calming Resets

1. Practice deep breathing
2. Reflect in silence
3. Write down your feelings
4. Tell your muscles to relax
5. Stand up and stretch
6. Take a slow walk
7. Draw something
8. Write down your feelings
9. Forgive someone
10. Listen to calming music

Boosting Resets

1. Jog in place
2. Run in place
3. Do jumping jacks
4. Drink a glass of water
5. Eat a healthy snack
6. Compliment someone
7. Help someone
8. Thank someone
9. Ask for help
10. Dance to upbeat music

These Numbers Have Names

Shockingly, about **90% of kids and teens in the United States** are never taught basic mental health skills at school, such as **how to cope with stress and anxiety** or **what to do if you feel depressed**.[5] These life skills are not part of the core curriculum. We assume that kids are learning these skills at home, but many of them never do, leaving them with a huge disadvantage in life. Sadly, the current mental health system in schools is highly reactive and primarily geared for at-risk students with severe behavioral problems or with diagnosable mental illnesses.

The U.S. Department of Behavioral Health estimates that 20% of teens live with a diagnosable mental illness, and yet only half of those students (meaning 10% of all students) will ever go on to get professional help.[6]

Compounding the problem, schools are understaffed for this reactionary model. The current ratio of students to school psychologists is a staggering **1,400 to 1**, and the ratio for school counselors is nearly **500 to 1**.[7] Even if schools hire more mental health workers, the model will still be reactive, and the vast majority of students will remain unserved. At Reset Schools, we believe mental health should be part of the core curriculum in schools, and we are committed helping make it a reality. Please join us in the movement at https://ResetSchools.org!

18.1 – Discussion Questions

1. What are some of your default coping mechanisms for dealing with stress? You can describe healthy or unhealthy coping skills.

2. Take 60 seconds to practice one of the Calming Resets and discuss how the activity made you feel afterward. What other activities can you add to the list?

3. Take 60 seconds to practice one of the Boosting Resets and discuss how the activity made you feel afterward. What other activities can you add to the list?

18.2 – Biofeedback

 Hey friends! Dr. OH here, back again to talk about a very cool approach to coping with struggles like stress, anxiety, and depression. This technique is something you can practice casually on your own (I know, because I do). That makes it a great candidate for dealing with mental speed bumps when you're on the go or in public.

The technique is called biofeedback. If you inspect the word "biofeedback," you can probably already guess what it is. Bio is having to do with your body (biology). Now combine that with feedback and there you have it – biofeedback involves using feedback from your body to understand the connection between your brain and body and the control that you can have over that connection.

The Brain-Body Connection

Our bodies can be hit hard by the physical consequences of anxiety and stress. For example, anxiety tends to provoke an elevated heart rate. Imagine you're hooked up to a heart monitor, and you're thinking about something stressful. You see your heart rate increasing on the monitor as you get more and more anxious.

Then you start breathing – slow, deep breaths – in and out through your nose (you can try it right now as you're reading!). When you inhale, you push all of the air to your stomach before filling your lungs. As you slowly exhale, you give yourself time to relax the muscles in your body. With each exhalation, you focus on relaxing a different set of muscles: your face, your arms, your shoulders, your hands, and so on. As you go through this process, you see your heart rate immediately affected by this ritual. Each breath brings you closer to your resting heartrate. The momentary lapse in thinking about the stressful topic opens up your ability to refocus and start fresh. In short, you have used the connection between your brain and body to alleviate a symptom of stress.

You are in Control

There are lots of fitness trackers like Fitbits and smartwatches that can help you monitor your heart rate, and some fitness companies are even developing software and hardware to help identify when you're stressed.[8] But you don't "have to have" a fancy device to practice biofeedback. It starts with being mindful of what your body is already trying to tell you. Eventually, biofeedback techniques can help you develop confidence in the control that you have over your physical and mental state. You will know the effect that you're having on your body's systems, and that knowledge is a huge part of what it takes to manage your mental health and wellbeing.

Biofeedback is a great tool to help you manage symptoms of anxiety, depression, ADHD, PTSD, digestive disorders, and many other stressors. To learn more, check out this article: www.verywellmind.com/what-is-biofeedback-2794875.[9]

18.2 – Discussion Questions

1. What types of feedback do you get from your body when you're in stressful situations? Think about things like increased heart rate, fast breathing, stomach discomfort, sweating, shaking.

2. What is the technique of biofeedback, and how can it help you manage your stress-related symptoms?

3. What are some ways you can develop your biofeedback skills?

18.3 – How to Resolve Conflict (Yikes!)

Sometimes the closest people in our support system will let us down, hurt us, or disappoint us. The same is true for us. Since we're not perfect, we will inevitably do things are hurtful... even by accident. As my mentor, Mrs. Burdick, said to our English class many years ago, **"We tend to hurt the most, the people we love the most."**

What?!! On the surface, that doesn't sound right! But as we look deeper, it starts to makes sense: the closest people in our life see all sides of us because we are with them more than anyone else. They're with us in our best moments: when we're loving, caring, and nurturing, and they're with us in our worst moments: when we're tired, cranky, and sometimes even mean.

Of course, the goal should always be to become more mentally healthy over time, leading to a more kindness and less conflict. But again: since perfection is unattainable, it is only wise to learn how to resolve conflict in a healthy way. (See Dr. Kirleen's section in Chapter 5.3.)

Conflict is a necessary part of life that we all experience. Learning how to resolve and cope with it is difficult for everyone, including adults. It can be easy for our emotions to get the best of us, especially if the conflict involves something we're passionate about. Thankfully, there are steps we can take to manage our emotions and work toward healthier relationships.[10]

Step 1. Process Your Emotions

As Dr. Kirleen pointed out in Chapter 15, anger is a secondary emotion. When we're hurt we tend to resort to anger to protect ourselves. Often, we are subconsciously reacting to something deeper, like feeling scared, hurt, disrespected, or trapped.[11]

Take time to process what happened and how it made you feel using the **RULER** method from Chapter 7. You really can learn to **Recognize, Understand, Label, Express,** and **Regulate** your emotions.

Are you hurt, scared, disappointed, misunderstood? If you're flooded with emotions, you're not in a good state to try and resolve a conflict.

It takes time to process your feelings, but it's so worth it! So don't suppress them. Process them. As you start to **Regulate** your emotions, you're already moving into Step 2 on the next page.

Step 2. Take Time to Reset

Do one of the **calming resets** (from earlier in this chapter) to emotion-down, or one of the **boosting resets** to emotion-up and feel energized. It takes practice to discover which coping skills work best for you.

As you're doing the reset activity, start to visualize a positive outcome. When you're in the middle of conflict, it can be hard to think past being right, but take a moment to visualize an outcome that would benefit everyone. How would you feel to walk away with a solution that made everyone happy? Reset strategies can take as little as 60 seconds or as long as you need them to be effective. Don't be afraid to take plenty of time so you can face the conflict calmly.[12]

Step 3. Check Your Motives

Once you've processed your emotions and taken time to reset, examine your motives by asking yourself the following 10 questions:

1. Is this something small I can overlook, or does it need to be addressed?

2. Do I need to establish any healthy boundaries here?

3. Am I trying to prove something here? Do I need to prove I'm right?

4. Do I have unfair expectations that they will automatically see things my way?

5. Am I open to listening to their version of events?

6. If I don't meet with them, will I later regret it? Will it create weirdness?

7. If I do meet with them, and it doesn't go great, how will I respond?

8. How could meeting with them affect the rest of my day, week, or month?

9. Do I feel safe enough to address this conflict, or should I involve an adult?

10. Will I be able to walk away and be okay, no matter the outcome?

As you consider your motives and the potential outcomes, you can make a wise **go/no-go** decision. Remember: even if you call a **no-go**, your emotions are still 100% valid, and it might be time to set some healthy emotional boundaries.

Step 4. Calmly Express Yourself

If you make the choice to talk about the conflict with the other person, you're really expressing that the relationship matters to you… which hopefully means the other person cares about you too. Your goal should be to clear up any misunderstandings and clarify expectations for the future. **If you're not open to the idea** that there could be additional facts you've missed or misunderstandings between the two of you, **then you're really not trying to resolve anything.** You're just trying to be right.[13]

Get to your main point early in the conversation, and give them a chance to respond. Don't make them nervous by beating around the bush. You came there to say something or to ask them something, so get it out on the table. Waiting only makes it worse for everyone.

Own your feelings for what happened, and state them clearly. Try not to assume you know their motives for what happened. Remain open to their thoughts and ideas. Even if the other person doesn't fight fair, don't take the bait. If they feel backed in a corner, they may get defensive and say something rude. Or perhaps they'll powerplay you with *"A lot of other people feel the same as me."* Just stay calm. Remember: you can remain under control, even if someone else is out of control. You can even be firm without being mean back.

Once you have expressed yourself and listened to the other person, talk about your needs. What do you need to feel right about the situation or to prevent it from happening again? Avoid language that sounds accusatory. This keeps the other person from feeling defensive. Don't forget to actively listen to the other person's needs. They deserve to be heard.

Step 5. Collaborate, Compromise, and Resolve

It's important to think of yourself and the other person as teammates when resolving a conflict. You may not agree with each other in the moment, but you're on the same team – the team of the relationship. Working together towards a common goal is called collaborating. As you give a little, and they give a little, it builds deep relational bonds. Both of you can start to let your guard down.

That's the sweet spot. That's when you realize it was never about being right. In this tender moment, you can begin to discuss how to handle similar situations in the future. You're coming to a compromise, an agreement you both feel good about. Collaborating and compromising are life skills that can take you far, especially when resolving conflict.[14] Try to end the conversation on a more positive note. This shows you want to move on and built up the relationship.

18.3 – Discussion Questions

1. Do you think it's true that we tend to hurt the most, the people we love the most? Why or why not?

2. What are some of hardest parts about conflict with family or a close friend?

3. Which of the **Check Your Motives** questions sticks out to you the most?

4. What would you do if you met with a close friend or family member to resolve a conflict, and they threw everything back on you?

5. Is it ever appropriate to set emotional boundaries? Why or why not?

Chapter 18 References

[1] Morin, A. (2020, April 3). *Healthy Coping Skills for Uncomfortable Emotions.* Verywell Mind. https://www.verywellmind.com/forty-healthy-coping-skills-4586742.

[2] *Coping Mechanisms.* GoodTherapy.org Therapy Blog. https://www.goodtherapy.org/blog/psychpedia/coping-mechanisms.

[3] Noble, L. J., Souza, R. R., & McIntyre, C. K. (2019, January). *Vagus Nerve Stimulation as a Tool for Enhancing Extinction in Exposure-Based Therapies.* U.S. National Library of Medicine. Psychopharmacology. https://www.ncbi.nlm.nih.gov/pmc/articles/PMC6368475/.

[4] Fuller, K. (2020, June 1). *An Indispensable List of Coping Skills Everyone Should Know About.* Fuller Life Counseling Partners. https://www.fullerlifecounseling.org/post/indispensable-list-of-coping-skills.

[5] *Data and Statistics on Children's Mental Health.* Centers for Disease Control and Prevention. (2020, June 15). https://www.cdc.gov/childrensmentalhealth/data.html.

[6] *Mental Health at School Infographics.* Mental Health First Aid. (2018, July 31). https://www.mentalhealthfirstaid.org/mental-health-at-school-infographics/.

[7] *Mental Health By the Numbers.* NAMI - National Alliance on Mental Illness. https://www.nami.org/mhstats.

[8] Eadicicco, L. (2020). New Smartwatch Tells How Stressed You Are. *Business Insider.* Retrieved from https://www.businessinsider.com/fitbit-sense-smartwatch-announced-stress-tracking-apple-watch-2020-8.

[9] Cherry, K. (2019). What Is Biofeedback and How Does It Work? *Verywellmind.com.* Retrieved from https://www.verywellmind.com/what-is-biofeedback-2794875.

[10] Taylor, J. (2019, August 29). *3 Keys to Resolving Conflict.* Psychology Today. https://www.psychologytoday.com/us/blog/the-power-prime/201908/3-keys-resolving-conflict.

[11] Psychology Tools: What is Anger? A Secondary Emotion. (2016, December 24) https://healthypsych.com/psychology-tools-what-is-anger-a-secondary-emotion/.

[12] Cochran, K. (2016). The development of conflict resolution skills in children: Preschool to adolescence. American Psychological Association. https://psycnet.apa.org/record/2000-07807-015

[13] Fiorillo, K., Louie, K., Kovac, S., & McCormack, C. *Tips For Managing Conflict Resolution At Home.* EverydayHealth.com. https://www.everydayhealth.com/healthy-living/healthy-home/tips-managing-conflict-resolution-home/.

[14] Department of Health & Human Services. (2014, August 21). *Family Conflict.* Better Health Channel. https://www.betterhealth.vic.gov.au/health/healthyliving/family-conflict.

Chapter 19

SUICIDE PREVENTION

19.1 – Teen Suicide Prevention

Hey everybody, Tom Thelen here. Teen suicide is a very sensitive topic. Some people even think talking about it will accidentally encourage more teens to end their own lives. Thankfully, research shows the opposite is true: talking with teens about the risks of suicide and showing them how to get help actually works... it reduces the risks of suicide. The National Council for Behavioral Health has an eight-hour training program called Youth Mental Health First Aid, and I am honored to be one of their certified trainers. In Mental Health First Aid, we show people how to help teens who are in a mental health crisis, such as having a panic attack or having suicidal thoughts. Mental Health First Aid is an evidence-based program for reducing suicide and for helping teens improve their mental health.[1] Rather than staying silent about suicide, loving adults (like me) need to commit to helping teens who are in crisis, and loving teenagers (like you) need to learn how to get help (when needed) and how to help your friends. That's what this chapter is all about.

I've Been There

As a teen, I experienced suicidal thoughts starting around 9th grade, and it got worse in 10th grade. My family relationships were strained, I was struggling in school, and I was battling anxiety and depression (although, I didn't know all of that at the time). Thankfully, 10th grade was also the year I connected with my English Teacher, Mrs. Burdick. She quickly became my trusted adult – the person I could talk to without feeling judged. She helped me get over my fear of asking for help, and eventually I got into counseling. It was a huge help! The wisdom I learned back then became the seeds of hope that grew in my heart for many years. It wasn't an overnight change, but in time... I became a new person.

Sadly, about ten years ago I lost a close friend to suicide, and that really rocked my world. At the time I mistakenly thought suicide only affected the most at-risk, depressed, isolated people, but that's simply not the case. Suicide can affect anyone in any type family… even the people who seem the most mentally healthy. That's why we try to use the phrase *"died by suicide"* rather than *"committed suicide."* We never know what was going on in someone's mind at the moment they ended their life, so we shouldn't judge them or their families.

As a public speaker, I've met many families who have lost loved ones to suicide, and most of them are made up of wholesome, loving, caring family members. I often hear that they simply didn't see any warning signs before it happened, and then it was too late. The person was thriving, excelling at school and in sports, and yet somehow they still died. We don't always have answers for the "why" behind suicide.

12 Protective Factors for Teen Suicide

Before we talk about the risk factors for suicide (meaning the warning signs and symptoms), I want to show you **12 Protective Factors** that are proven to reduce the risks of teen suicide:[2]

1. Having a close connection with a trusted adult
2. Getting exercise, eating healthy, and sleeping well
3. Having a supportive home life
4. Having economic stability (enough money)
5. Having supportive friends
6. Being part of a community
7. Attending school regularly
8. Having high self-esteem
9. Being resilient and "bouncing back"
10. Feeling in control of your life
11. Spirituality
12. Avoiding drugs and alcohol

When we teach Mental Health First Aid, we explain that every teen needs many of these positive influences and healthy choices in their life. That being said, there is one protective factor that has been proven to be the most effective at reducing teen suicide. Take a look at the list above… which one do you think it is?

Research shows the number one, most protective factor for reducing the risks of teen suicide is (drumroll please) **having a close connection with at least one**

trusted adult. (Yup… I listed it as number one for a reason.) Back when I was a teen I didn't realize it, but the connection I made with Mrs. Burdick was more powerful than having high self-esteem, resiliency, or anything else on the list. Honestly, that relationship probably saved my life. I know it saved my heart.

The Recent Rise in Teen Suicide

I believe your generation has it harder than my generation… at least from a mental health perspective. All the numbers show that teen anxiety, depression, and suicide rates have been increasing since the mid-2000s. In October of 2019 the Centers for Disease Control published a new study on teen suicide. It showed that from 2007 to 2017 the suicide rate for young people ages 10 to 14 in the United States **NEARLY TRIPLED**.[3] Did you catch that? That's almost three times as many suicides in only 10 years. You might be thinking, *"But wait… was suicide already going up, year after year?"* The answer is no. The same study by the CDC showed that suicide rates for the same age group had been declining between 2000 and 2007. Back in 2007, the leading causes of death for teens in the U.S. were as follows: **#1 – accidental deaths** (like car crashes), followed by **#2 – homicide** (such as murder), followed by **#3 – suicide** (ending your own life). Today, suicide is the **second leading cause of death** for teens in the U.S. I hope those numbers are alarming to you. They certainly are to me.[4]

You might be asking, ***"What happened? Why did teen suicide rise so quickly and so steadily?"*** I don't think we can pin 100% of the blame at any one single cause, but I'm also not afraid to talk about the ***possible causes***. We need to use common sense and talk about the elephant in the room. What happened in 2007?

2007 was the birth of the smartphone and the start of the social media boom. Before 2007, no one had a smartphone in their pocket, and by the end of 2017 practically everyone did.

If I were you, I'd probably be thinking, **"Here we go again, another adult blaming phones!"**

Stay with me here. I'm not blaming phones.

I love phones, and I use mine all the time. I also use social media, and yes… I hope you'll follow me at @bullyingspeaker. That's a shameless plug, and I don't mind making it.

What I'm saying is: it's not the phones – it's how we use them. It's the ironic social isolation that ***can be caused*** by too much social media, gaming, and screen time. It's the addiction, the anxiety, and the depression. It's the FOMO (fear of missing out). It's the envy and the jealousy that ***can happen*** when we misuse our phones and let them misuse our brains.[5]

At the same time, phones can be a huge benefit to our mental health! Phone and technology can keep us connected to our friends and loved ones. Many of us have online friendships and communities that dramatically enrich our lives. It's common sense that phones and social media can even help prevent suicide… if we use them wisely.

It's not a "phone = bad" conversation. It's a simple reminder that we need to keep our phone usage in check. We should track our screen time, set reasonable limits, and ask friends and family members to help keep us accountable. We need to press pause in our minds, so we can have a mental "reset." We need a reality check and a self-evaluation. We cannot let ourselves become addicted, and we should never let phones replace our need for in-person connection. That's just the truth.

As Dr. OH has pointed out, you're going to be more emotional as a teenager, and heightened emotions can cloud your better judgement. You may not know when to put down the phone. The rational part of the brain (the prefrontal cortex) is still being developed. It's normal for your teen years to feel like a rollercoaster, so you need to hang on for dear life as you ride through the highs and lows. Every other teen is also experiencing extreme highs and lows, even if they never show the lows, and even if they only post their highs on social media. In the meantime, take a deep breath and hang in there. Cling to your support system, your trusted adults, and every other protective factor available because clearly… it's going to be a wild ride.

Get Help Right Away

If you or one of your friends is having thoughts of suicide, and especially if it is being discussed as an option, you need to talk with a trusted adult right away. I can't say it more clearly! Even if your friend tells you not to tell anyone, you still need to do what's best for your friend. **If it's an emergency, call 911 right away.** Better to risk the friendship than to risk the life of your friend. You can also call or text the **National Suicide Prevention Lifeline at 988,** and someone will be there for you 24-hours a day. **YOU CAN GET HELP** even when you're at your lowest low. The best days of your life are still ahead of you. I really believe that, and I believe in you.

19.1 – Discussion Questions

1. What are some of the common misconceptions about suicide, and how do these inaccurate ideas contribute to the stigma around suicide?

2. Read through each of the **12 Protective Factors** again and discuss how each can help prevent teen suicide.

3. Take out a fresh piece of paper, and write the names of the most trusted adults in your life. Be default, we're talking about your parents or guardians You need safe, nonjudgmental adults who will listen to you and help out if you're ever in a crisis. If you can't talk to an adult in your home, ask to talk with your school counselor or school psychologist.

4. Let's have a debate. Who can present a point of view for the question: how much screen time is too much screen time? And after that... who can respectfully present a different opinion?

5. **Personal Reflection Journal:** Ask yourself the deep questions posed by Tom in this section. Am I at risk of harming myself or anyone else? I anyone else I know at risk? If so, what should I do about it, and who should I talk to? How much time am I spending on my phone? How much screen time is too much for my own mental health? How can I set reasonable limits and be held accountable? What are some healthy uses of technology that build up my mental health?

19.2 – Suicide Warning Signs & Prevention

Hey guys! It's Dr. Kirleen here to continue the difficult conversation on teen suicide. Death of any kind is always hard to understand and talk about, suicide even more so. But like most things in life, once you talk about it, you feel more empowered to address the issue head-on. So, even though this can be a touchy topic, it's crucial for us to keep it real and have a conversation about how suicide can affect you or someone you love. It's even more important to know when to ask for help or get help for someone. As we discuss this topic, I want you to think of a trusted adult (a parent, neighbor, teacher, or school counselor) you can reach out to if some of this stuff starts to hit home.

Triggers of Teen Stress

How many times have you thought, "I'm so stressed out"? Well, if you're like most teens, the answer is probably "a lot." Stress levels usually rise and fall, depending on the circumstances around you. But high-stress levels over a long period can lead to depression, and depression is one of the leading risk factors for suicide.[6] It is essential to identify and manage your stress triggers. One the next page, we'll discuss five common triggers for teen stress.

1. **Academic Stress:** Teens who succeed in school, as well as teens who struggle with school, often build their identity around school success or failure. Class ranking systems and advanced placement classes make the pressure to succeed even more intense. There is nothing wrong with excelling academically. But when your self-worth revolves around your achievements or lack of achievements, you can experience depression and other negative emotions. Academic stress may lead teens to take on an "I don't care attitude" because they feel like they can't measure up. Some teens go in the total opposite direction and work their fingers to the bone, trying to get perfect grades. When you build an identity around high achievement, you tend to feel shame when you fail, and you can never fully live up to your standard of perfection. The only way to lose this shame is by talking about it! You are more than your academic success or failure, and you are more than what others think about you. Speak up and ask for help if you're struggling.

2. **Social Stress:** Some of the best parts of being a teen are getting to hang out with your friends, participating in extracurricular activities, and dating for the first time. If these normal activities are full of drama or bring out insecurities, it can make social situations unbearable. Social stress can be more difficult if you have social anxiety. Social anxiety is an intense, persistent fear of being watched and judged by others. This fear can affect school and your other day-to-day activities.[7] Learning how to deal with social stress is part of growing up, and most teens have moments where they feel weird or awkward socially. Sharing how you feel with close friends and trusted adults can make a huge difference.

3. **Negative Self Talk:** 12,000 to 60,000 thoughts run through our minds every day. Most of them are repetitive thoughts we use to get through life, but many of those thoughts can be negative. Negative self-talk can speak to your core beliefs about yourself. Core beliefs are the foundation of your self-esteem, and if those beliefs are negative, you could quickly spiral into bad mental health. Having an abundance of negative self-talk can lead to dwelling on mistakes and feeling defined by any shortcomings. Instead of embracing issues and mistakes as learning experiences, you chalk them up to your inabilities. People with negative core beliefs don't see their accomplishments, only their failures. Grown adults struggle with this, and it's even more difficult for teens. With societal and parental pressure mounting, take some time to evaluate your thoughts and your self-talk.

4. **Physical Appearance:** I'm sure you've had a friend or two who's made a comment about how they look, or maybe you've found yourself thinking I'm so fat, ugly, or average. As your body grows and changes, you can begin to feel self-conscious and hyper-aware of every blemish and extra pound.

Photoshopped images and heavily filtered posts on social media can make it impossible to measure up. Body image is someone's perception, thoughts, or attitude about the way their body looks. Negative body image can become so severe that it is harmful to your mental health. Negative body image is connected to low self-esteem, anxiety, depression, and eating disorders in teens. Taking the simple step of saying one positive thing about how you look every day can go a long way towards improving your body image.[8]

5. **Problems at Home:** Parents *"they just don't' understand."* If you like old school rap, you might remember that line from The Fresh Prince of Bellaire, aka: Will Smith. This rap lyric sums up what teens have felt for decades. Teenagers are in the natural progression of moving away from their parent's beliefs, and parents are trying to hold on to control. This combination can make home life feel unbearable. Sometimes teens feel that their values and opinions don't match up with their parents. It's normal to have differing beliefs, but this can make it hard for teens to have a safe place to express themselves without feeling judged. If you're struggling to open up to a parent, don't be afraid to talk to a teacher, school counselor, or even an aunt or neighbor. There are resources available specifically for teens who are struggling with their mental health. Advocate for yourself and your mental wellbeing!

Suicide Warning Signs & Risk Factors

Suicide warning signs can come in many different forms. The following list is not comprehensive, but it's a good starting point to understand the warning signs of suicide.

- Becoming extremely agitated, upset, depressed and/or anxious

- Beginning to use alcohol and/or drugs, or using them more frequently

- Changing obvious characteristics of your personality

- Being self-destructive or engaging in risk-taking behaviors

- Changes in sleeping, eating, or other patterns

- Expressing hopelessness or a feeling of being trapped with no way out

- Extreme mood swings

- Frequently talking about death or dying

- Giving away possessions for no particular reason

- Isolation and withdrawing from social contact, especially if it's sudden

- Looking for and/or acquiring means to commit suicide, such as getting a gun or a lot of medication

- Making a point to say goodbye to people

- Saying things like, "I wish I were dead," or "I wish I had never been born"

When to Get Help

If you're even remotely thinking *"maybe I should talk to someone,"* then it's time to get help from your parents, guardians, or another trusted adult! There's no shame in asking for help. It's a normal part of the teen years. A trusted adult can help you sort out your feelings and point you in the right direction. Sometimes just venting and expressing your throughs will help you feel better. Talking about suicide can feel awkward and maybe even a little overwhelming, but the more we share and talk about it, the more control we gain over the issues.

The most important thing you can do is to talk to a trusted adult (like one of your parents) when your emotions feel out of control. **You can also call or text the Suicide Prevention Lifeline at 988.** They are available 24/7, and they can help you get connected to a mental health professional.

19.2 – Discussion Questions

1. What are some examples of situations where a teen should reach out for help?

2. Name the trusted adults you will go to if you need to talk about your emotions or if you suspect one of your friends is having suicidal thoughts.

3. Examine the teen stressors we discussed (academic, social, negative self-talk, physical appearance, problems at home) which two are most likely to affect you and why? What tools do you currently use to reduce stress and what tool from the list of six discussed do you need to use more frequently?

4. Think about your own mental health, is there anything you need to share with your parents or another trusted adult? Do you feel that your mental health is good, average, or needing some improvement... and why?

19.3 – How to Help a Friend

Hi, it's Dr. Kagan again. Young people come to me all the time with emotional concerns about someone they know or their friend. They want guidance to help their friend. They are also unsure whether their friend is at-risk for dangerous activities like abusing drugs, self-harm, or suicide. I know it's scary, and you can feel helpless not knowing what to do when that friend confides in you. Tom already introduced you to Mental Health First Aid which can help you in these situations. It is important that you know the signs and symptoms of someone in emotional distress or experiencing a more serious mental health problem.[9] It's not always obvious what to do in the moment, but the good news is: we can give you some basic tools.

Dr. Kirleen and Tom gave you some great tools for suicide prevention, and I want you to use those skills for your own mental health and for any emergencies. Even if you suspect it might be an emergency, call 911 or call the hotline by dialing or texting 988, just to be sure. In this section, I want to talk more about **non-emergencies**. I want to give you some tools that can be used to provide basic help to others during times of distress when harm or suicide is not an immediate concern.

It's worth repeating that all of us can help a friend or someone you come in contact with who is in distress. You don't have to be a doctor to use a first-aid kit. If someone is bleeding, you give them a band-aid. If the bleeding doesn't stop, you call for help or call 911. Mental Health First Aid is a lot like that – it's a basic first-aid kit for the mind.

You're not there to play the role of doctor or physician (leave the serious work to the mental health professionals). You're there to support your friend, to make them feel cared for, to make sure they're safe, and to make sure they talk with a trusted adult (like a parent or a counselor) when needed.

You have such an important role! Can you just imagine how great it would be for us all to be equipped to provide mental health first aid, and help one another in times of emotional distress? Below are some important support tools you can use to help a friend.

7 Tools in Your Mental Health First Aid Kit

1. **Check for risk of harm**. If someone is talking about hurting themselves or someone else, take it seriously and report it immediately to a parent, guardian, trusted adult, **AND** to law enforcement. If you sense anyone is in danger, or if they're making a plan to hurt someone, call 911 right away!

2. **Be Present.** Perhaps the most important thing when providing emotional assistance is to be fully present and be a good listener. Being fully present means to put aside all your other agenda, needs, and activities in your own life and truly be there for the friend in need. Being a good listener involves listening to what your friend is feeling, their thoughts, and the circumstances or problems that have led to those feelings. Be there for them.

3. **Have empathy.** Acknowledge, accept, and validate their feelings with a nonjudgmental attitude. Use phrases like, "I hear you are very distressed" or "Wow, that is upsetting!" or just paraphrase why they are so upset. That is called ***active listening,*** and it shows that you hear them. Providing genuine empathy and validation can be so supportive for your friend.

4. **Don't play the expert.** Don't be so quick to give your opinion, recommendations, or advice. It's not easy to hold back on giving advice, but it often allows your friend in need to come up with their own ideas that will help them, and that is so much more beneficial. By just providing understanding, your friend can draw power and strength to help themself and become their own best advisor. Of course, you can eventually give helpful guidance and advice, especially if they ask for advice, or if they are considering ideas and actions that are not good for them.

5. **Maintain your own composure and wellness.** When there is a lot of drama and distress around you, it's easy to become immersed in that stress and feel overwhelmed. If that happens, don't try to take over, and don't think of yourself as the exclusive caretaker for your friend. That is unrealistic and destined to fail. To be a good helper you must be able to stay a little detached or removed from the situation. Maintain a mindset of being a supportive friend. You can still show true empathy for a friend without carrying the emotional weight of their drama or distress.

6. **Practice mental health together.** Participate with your friend in activities that promote mental health, wellness, and resiliency. Volunteer together, become work-out partners, share positive social experiences, enjoy fun clubs, sign up for activities that better the community, and participate in experiences that enhance mental health like yoga, meditation, and support groups. All this enhances your friendship and mutually supports each other's mental wellness.

7. **Get help when it is needed, even if your friend doesn't want help.** This circles back to point 1. Know when the situation is an emergency or when it is beyond your ability to help. That includes if your friend is at risk for hurting themself, engaging in dangerous activities, or is at-risk for suicide. In those situations, you must seek out a trusted adult, like a parent or a mental health professional immediately. If you are not sure, get help. If your friend asks and even pleads that you not tell anyone else, tell them you care too much for them and you must get them help. Offer to go with them. You don't want anything to happen which hurts your friend or puts them at risk.

This short article can't cover everything you need to know about helping someone in emotional distress, but I hope it offers you some tools to add to your mental health first aid kit, and I hope you feel ready to assist. If you want further training, speak to your school counselor or search online for Mental Health First Aid. You can even consider taking one of our Mental Health 101 Trainings online or hosting one of our live events at your school. Helping someone who is experiencing emotional distress is a wonderful act of kindness, and through your act of kindness you are making the world a better place!

19.3 – Discussion Questions

1. **Group Activity:** Role play a situation where a friend is in emotional distress. It could be related to an argument with parents or friends, getting a bad grade, a disappointing event, or just feeling poorly. In the role play ask a volunteer to play the distressed friend, the helping friend, and have the rest of the students observe.

2. Role play for 5 minutes, then debrief on the Mental Health First Aid tools that were used. What other tools could have been used?

3. Select new volunteers, pick a different stressful scenario, and repeat the role play. Give others an opportunity to participate in the role play and to make observations.

4. After the activity is done, use the space below to write a plan for how you will help your friends if they are ever in a mental health crisis.

If a friend of mine is in crisis, here are some things I can do to help:

-
-
-
-
-

Chapter 19 References

[1] National Council for Behavioral Health. (2016). Mental Health First Aid USA: For Adults Assisting Young People. Washington DC: National Council for Behavioral Health.

[2] Preventing Suicide | Violence Prevention | Injury Center | CDC. (2020, April 21). From https://www.cdc.gov/violenceprevention/suicide/fastfact.html.

[3] Curtin, S. C., & Heron, M. (2019, October 17). Death Rates Due to Suicide and Homicide Among Persons Aged 10–24: United States, 2000–2017. Centers for Disease Control. https://www.cdc.gov/nchs/products/databriefs/db352.htm.

[4] Suicide Statistics. (2020, July 29). From https://afsp.org/suicide-statistics/.

[5] Abi-Jaoude, E., Treurnicht Naylor, K., & Pignatiello, A. (2020, February 10). Smartphones, Social Media Use and Youth Mental Health. Annals of Global Health. https://www.ncbi.nlm.nih.gov/pmc/articles/PMC7012622/.

[6] Yang, L., Zhao, Y., Wang, Y., Liu, L., Zhang, X., Li, B., & Cui, R. (2015). The Effects of Psychological Stress on Depression. Current neuropharmacology, 13(4), 494–504. https://doi.org/10.2174/1570159x1304150831150507.

[7] Social Anxiety Disorder. Retrieved from. https://www.nimh.nih.gov/health/publications/social-anxiety-disorder-more-than-just-shyness/index.shtml.

[8] Neringa Antanaityte. (n.d.). From https://tlexinstitute.com/how-to-effortlessly-have-more-positive-thoughts/.

[9] Understanding Suicidal Ideation in Teens. Retrieved fromhttps://www.verywellmind.com/suicidal-ideation-defined-2611328.

Chapter 20

MENTAL CONDITIONS & DISORDERS

20.1 – Understanding and Acceptance

Hey, it's Tom again. Understanding and accepting ourselves, our peers, our friends, and family is an important aspect of mental health, but it can be very difficult when we're **unaware** of the challenges we ourselves face, much less the challenges other people may be facing. As a student, you should never assume that someone has a particular mental illness or disorder, but you should know a lot of people have them – it's possible you do too – and that's 100% cool. In Mental Health First Aid, we teach that 20% of teens have a diagnosable mental illness or disorder, but less than half of them ever get professional help (which to me, is a tragedy).

With *Mental Health 101*, our goal is to normalize the conversation around mental health, so more students are brave enough to speak up and get the help they need.

Knowing that so many people have mental disorders helps us be more graceful with everyone around us, hopefully even more graceful with how we see ourselves. It's true: many people around us are facing challenges we will never fully see or understand, and that alone helps us approach everyone with an attitude of grace and flexibility.

Keep in mind, our attitude is not: **"Those people…over there."** Our attitude is **"us" and "we."** We are all humans, and we all have infinite value. Just as we would never judge someone who wears glasses or hearing aids, we should never judge someone with a mental condition or disorder. Celebrating our differences and learning how to respect everyone is an important step in living a life of mental health. And here's the bonus: having an open mind towards people who are different than us allows us to be understood, as well. That's what I call a win-win.

What is a Mental Disorder?

Dr. OH gave a great definition and clear criteria for mental disorders in chapter 4, so let's do a recap. A mental disorder, also referred to as a mental illness, is a chemical imbalance in the brain that causes abnormal thoughts, behaviors, emotions, or perceptions. One common thread is that **mental disorders cause ongoing disruptions to the person's daily life,** and thus, professional help is needed.[1] Sometimes these symptoms account for random behaviors that are hard to understand. There are many different types of mental conditions and disorders ranging from mild to severe and from temporary to permanent. The good news is: almost all mental conditions and disorders are treatable with help from a doctor or mental health professional, like a counselor, psychologist, or psychiatrist. In the next section we will take a deeper look at some of the more common mental conditions and disorders.

20.1 – Discussion Questions

1.   In your own words, how would you define the term, "mental disorder?"

2.   How should we treat people with mental disorders or mental illnesses?

3.   How do you think mental disorders and conditions are different than learning disabilities? (If you don't know, that's ok. We're discussing it in chapter 22.)

20.2 – Common Mental Disorders (Part 1)

We've already devoted several sections of the book to some of the more common mental disorders, such as **PTSD in chapter 14, Major Depressive Order in chapter 16,** and **Generalized Anxiety Disorder in chapter 17**. In the next two sections, we're going to look at four more common mental disorders and their symptoms.[2]

Eating Disorders

Eating disorders often stem from an unhealthy focus on body weight, body image, and/or food intake. People who struggle with eating disorders tend to directly connect their physical image to their sense of self-worth. This causes them to be hyper-aware of their body, the food they eat, and how others see them. Eating disorders can cause serious physical side effects if gone untreated. Malnutrition, heart or kidney failure, and brain dysfunction are all common side effects of eating disorders. Other complications can include low bone density, tooth decay, brittle hair and nails, and dehydration. In extreme cases, heart failure and other complications can lead to death.[3]

People who struggle with eating disorders can be **underweight, overweight, or in the normal weight range,** so it is not exclusive to any particular body type. Eating disorders occur in four percent of girls and two percent of boys, though the number of boys coming forward about their eating disorder is growing. People with eating disorders may experience one or more other mental illnesses like anxiety, depression, or suicidal ideation.[4]

Some symptoms of eating disorders include:

- Excessively restrictive dieting or fasting
- Binge eating
- Persistent vomiting or use of laxatives
- Lying about food intake
- Obsessive rituals or habits around meals
- Obsessive behavior around body shape (weighing, measuring, checking)
- Anxiety, depression, or irritability
- Social withdrawal
- Feelings of guilt, shame, or self-hate

On average, three percent of adolescents are diagnosed with an eating disorder, but experts believe the real number to be much higher because so many people hide the conditions from their loved ones.[3]

Like most mental conditions, eating disorders can be treated by a mental health professional. Common treatments involve counseling, family therapy, and physical interventions. With long term treatment, eating disorders can be managed, and full recovery is possible.

Obsessive Compulsive Disorder (OCD)

Obsessive Compulsive Disorder (OCD) is an anxiety disorder where intrusive thoughts and compulsions cause behaviors that interfere with daily life and activities. People tend to joke about someone having OCD if they see a person who is organized or very particular about certain things, but that kind of joking is unfair, and it minimizes the conversation around OCD. Diagnosable OCD is much more debilitating and is not a joking matter. Some obsessions commonly associated with OCD include fear of germs or disease, fear of the loss of a loved one, fear of physical injury, and many more.[5]

People with OCD often use compulsive behaviors to keep intrusive thoughts at bay. In extreme cases, these compulsive behaviors make it impossible to function in society. Some of these obsessive and compulsive behaviors include:

- Excessive washing or bathing

- Constantly checking doors and windows

- Repeating prayers or words of affirmation to ensure safety or health

- The need for symmetry or order

- Touching things a specific number of times

- A rigid routine that takes up large amounts of time

One common treatment for OCD is Exposure/Response Therapy where patients are exposed to their intrusive thoughts without giving in to the compulsive behavior. Recovery is possible, and even probable with professional mental health treatment.[5] Therapy, combined with medication can allow people with OCD to recover and live high-functioning, successful lives.

20.2 – Discussion Questions

1. If you suspected that a friend of yours was suffering from an eating disorder, would you treat them any differently? How would you help your friend?

2. Teens often joke around about OCD, especially when they see someone behaving in a quirky way. Is this a fair subject to joke about? How would you feel if you suffered from OCD, and people around you were always making jokes about it?

3. What are some positive ways to speak up when we hear a person making jokes about mental conditions or disorders?

20.3 – Common Mental Disorders (Part 2)

Bipolar Disorder

Bipolar disorder (also called manic depression) occurs when extreme shifts in mood, energy, and concentration occur on a regular basis causing an ongoing disruption to daily life. These mood swings range from extremely positive and hyperactive to the exact opposite: extremely depressed moods with little to no energy. These extreme conditions can last for days, weeks, or even months.

People with bipolar disorder can experience intense emotions whether positive or negative. Some symptoms of bipolar disorder include:

- Feeling very energized, excited, or jumpy
- Feeling very depressed or low
- Trouble sleeping
- Loss of appetite
- Weight loss or weight gain
- Moving or talking very slowly (or very quickly)
- Racing thoughts and trouble concentrating
- Feeling as if you can do many things at once
- Trouble completing simple tasks
- Risky behavior like excessive spending, eating, or drinking
- Inability to experience pleasure

Bipolar disorder is all about extreme shifts between the highs and lows. There is very little middle ground. Some of the more common treatments for Bipolar disorder include medication and therapy or counseling.

People who get professional treatment for bipolar disorder often recover and return to a more stable mental state.[6]

Schizophrenia

Schizophrenia causes individuals to lose touch with reality which affects their thoughts, feelings, and behavior. People with Schizophrenia and their loved ones can be greatly affected by the symptoms of this mental health disorder.[7] Persistent schizophrenia without treatment can make functioning in society nearly impossible. Some of the common symptoms include:

- Hallucinations that affect all five senses (hearing voices is the most common)
- Mental delusions that seem like reality, but are not reality
- Persistent trouble concentrating
- Jumbled speech
- Depression
- Paranoia (extreme irrational fears)

Treating schizophrenia varies from person to person, but anti-psychotic medication, counseling, and psychotherapy can ease the symptoms and allow those with Schizophrenia to recover and function effectively in the world.

Wrap Up

It's important to normalize the conversation around mental health by treating everyone equally, refusing to pass judgment, and refraining from joking about mental illness. When we suspect that we, or someone we know, may be suffering from a mental illness or disorder, we need to talk about it openly and honestly with a licensed mental health professional, like a counselor, psychologist, or psychiatrist. If we are prescribed mental health medications, we need to take our medicine just as openly as we would take any other kind of medication, knowing it is 100% necessary for our total health and wellbeing. And if people don't understand or accept us for who we are, then that's on them. They're missing out.

20.3 – Discussion Questions

1. What are some of the symptoms of bipolar disorder?

2. What are some of the symptoms of schizophrenia? (And which one is the most common?)

3. If you suspected that you might be suffering from either bipolar disorder or schizophrenia, what would you do? Who would you go to for help?

Chapter 20 References

[1] World Health Organization. Mental Disorders. 2019, www.who.int/news-room/fact-sheets/detail/mental-disorders.

[2] National Collaborating Centre for Mental Health (UK). "Common Mental Health Disorders." Common Mental Health Disorders: Identification and Pathways to Care., U.S. National Library of Medicine, 1 Jan. 1970, www.ncbi.nlm.nih.gov/books/NBK92254/.

[3] National Council for Behavioral Health. (2016). Mental Health First Aid USA: For Adults Assisting Young People. Washington DC: National Council for Behavioral Health.

[4] Eating Disorders in Adolescence. (2018, April 18). Retrieved July 20, 2020, from https://www.hhs.gov/ash/oah/news/e-updates/april-2018-eating-disorders/index.html.

[5] Clifton, C., & Price, J. (2020, December 3). *Living with OCD*. International OCD Foundation. https://iocdf.org/ocd-finding-help/living-with-ocd/.

[6] "Bipolar Disorder." National Institute of Mental Health, U.S. Department of Health and Human Services, 2020, www.nimh.nih.gov/health/topics/bipolar-disorder/index.shtml.

[7] "Schizophrenia." National Institute of Health, U.S. Dept of Health and Human Services, 2020, www.nimh.nih.gov/health/topics/schizophrenia/index.shtml.

Chapter 21

AUTISM

21.1 – What is Autism Spectrum Disorder?

Hello again, everyone! Dr. Kagan here. Have you heard about autism, autistic individuals, Autism Spectrum Disorder (ASD) or Asperger's Disorder? Or maybe you have autism or Asperger's Syndrome or someone in your family does. Maybe you know somebody in your school or in your classes that has autism or Asperger's Syndrome. By the way, **be comfortable using the word autism, autism spectrum,** or **Asperger's Syndrome**.[1] These terms are widely used and people with autism or Asperger's Disorder[2] often choose these terms to describe themselves. Of course, everyone has a right to decide how they want to be described or characterized so, if you are not sure, ask the person. After all, a key theme in this book is to get rid of the shame, embarrassment and stigma of any label and respect all people for who they are.

Our hope and aspiration are that people with autism value who they are, feel good about themselves, and that all people feel that way about people with autism or Asperger's Disorder and do not judge them because of a label.

Professionally speaking, Autism Spectrum Disorder is a condition related to brain development that impacts how a person experiences and socializes with others. Autism can cause problems in social interaction and communication. People with Autism may seem socially awkward. Some make poor eye contact. That is, they have difficulties gazing at you in the usual way that people look at each other when they are speaking. It can also result in limited and repetitive patterns of behavior, like being obsessed with Disney characters or anime'. The term "spectrum" in Autism Spectrum Disorder refers to the wide range of symptoms and severity. Some people with autism have intellectual and learning disabilities. Other people with autism do not.

Doctor's once thought that Asperger's Syndrome was a separate condition from autism but today Asperger's Syndrome is technically no longer a diagnosis and is a part of Autism Spectrum Disorder.[3]

Nevertheless, lots of people still use the term Asperger's Syndrome, understand it as a form of Autism Spectrum Disorder and often the individual is "high functioning" or intellectually and academically capable. Many young people with so-called Asperger's Syndrome are in mainstream or regular classes because they can handle the curriculum and the learning demands of regular classes. It is the social aspects of school and life that are challenging.

Like any diagnosis, only a trained professional like a doctor or mental health specialist can establish whether a person has autism. Some people with autism struggle with a lot of anxiety and depression because it is so difficult to "fit in" especially with their peers. Experts say that 1 in 59 children are living with autism. Chances are, you know someone with autism or have a classmate with autism. It is nothing anyone can catch; it is not contagious! Researchers believe one is born with autism and it is thought to be genetic, which means a gene gets passed on to you by your parents that causes autism, just like your physical features, aspects of your personality and some medical conditions. There is so much more information about autism, and I suggest you go to a website that has a good reputation like KidsHealth.org, to learn more.[4]

Focus on the Positives

But let us not just focus on the problems. Let us focus on the positives, as well.[5] As a psychologist, I have found that people who have autism have opened new doors for me; sharing new insights, are often not tied to social pressures like being the most popular and do not get into all that negative drama of who's cool and who is not. It is often a breath of fresh air.

Take my young friend Billy who had autism. (I changed his name to protect his privacy.) Billy and his family had settled on describing his condition as Asperger's Syndrome. He was always honest and so authentic. If you knew Billy, you loved him for his kindness, his caring ways, and his many talents. He was a great snowboarder, he made wool hats by hand, he could weave different materials to make bookmarks and wonderful handicrafts, and he was so smart. He went to college. And while he did well in college, the social and academic pressures were overwhelming, at times. Billy understood what it was like to be different and he empathized with those who struggled like he did. As a teenager and young man in his 20's, he saved money to donate to an organization that serves people with developmental disabilities. Autism sometimes made Billy's life difficult. He wanted so badly to have friends and a girlfriend, but he was very socially awkward, and it was challenging for him to establish relationships despite his efforts. Billy was a great friend!

So, there are so many positives and why not open your friends' circle to new possibilities. I promise you it will be enjoyable, rewarding, and you will learn about the gift of being kind and giving of yourself.

21.1 – Discussion Questions

1. In your own words how would you describe the characteristics, strengths and challenges of living with autism and Asperger's Syndrome.

2. How do you know what characteristics are related to autism or are just part of his/her/your personality?

21.2 – Three Functional Levels of Autism

Hey everybody, Tom here. Kids and teens with autism spectrum disorder are often diagnosed as functioning at one of three levels. The three levels help mental health professionals understand and communicate more effectively about the diagnosis – **but they are never meant to label people.** The levels are often referred to as **mild (level one), moderate (level two), and severe (level three).** Many people with autism have a core, most noticeable symptom along with other verbal, social, or intellectual challenges. However, it is important to understand that each person is unique, along with their diagnosis. When doctors and psychologists assess people with autism and refer to their level, the goal is to better understand and treat their diagnosis. The levels also give a broad starting point for how we can better understand, relate, and interact with people on the autism spectrum.[6]

The three levels represent verbal abilities, adaptability, social skills, expanding interest, and the ability to manage day-to-day life. It is common for those with autism to have their diagnosis level changed based on the progressing skills. School psychologists can help make these assessments by working with students with autism and tracking their progress in each area.[7]

Autism Spectrum Level One

The first level of the autism spectrum is considered **the mildest level**. This level requires the least amount of support, but support is still essential in the success of the autistic person. Someone on level one of the autism spectrum may have difficulty keeping up friendships and relating in conversations. They may want to do things their way and keep a strict routine. Having repetitive or restrictive habits is normal for this level, but this behavior is often mild. Even though they may struggle with social cues and conversation, they can still have functional relationships and social interaction, even if it doesn't come naturally to them.[8]

Autism Spectrum Level Two

The second level of autism is used to describe people who need a moderate level support. This level is seen as an intermittent or middle level of autism. Those who meet the criteria for level two need more support than level one, but less support than level three. Their social skills are usually less advanced than level one. They may or may not communicate verbally, and when they do it may be short sentences on a single topic.

People on the second level may be noticeably different than their peers. They may struggle with making eye contact, showing emotion, or responding to social ques. Typically, their habits or repetitive behaviors are very important to them, and they may become upset or uncomfortable if they are interrupted (BS. Abrahams et al.).

Autism Spectrum Level Three

The third level of the autism spectrum requires the most support. It is considered the most severe level of the spectrum. Most people in level three are either nonverbal (meaning they do not talk) or they have a very limited vocabulary. Some are taught to use an iPad or a tablet to communicate by pointing at the pictures. Typically, their restrictive and repetitive habits, such as making noise, spinning, rocking, or other behaviors make it more difficult for them to function with daily activities.

People in level three can struggle with schedule changes or unexpected events. They may also have difficulty with sensory overload, meaning bright lights or loud sounds can cause them discomfort. The third level of autism requires a great deal of support for individuals to learn functional life skills (BS. Abrahams et al., 2017).

Respecting People on the Autism Spectrum

When interacting with someone who has autism, regardless of where they are on the spectrum, they might sound and act differently than you do. Instead of pinpointing or being intimidated by these differences, try to put yourself in their shoes. Struggling to communicate can make it difficult to socialize or make friends, so be understanding when interacting with those who are autistic. The quote from autism expert, Dr. Barry M. Prizant (which is on the next page), is a great example of what it's like for people with autism to interact socially.

> "The most significant trust-related challenge for people with autism is trusting other people. Most of us are neurologically hardwired with the ability to predict the behavior of others—to read body language intuitively and make subconscious judgments based on how relaxed a person's body is, on how a person looks at other people, or by the social context. But that is often more difficult for people with autism."[9] – Dr. Barry M. Prizant

Do your best to be patient with people on the autism spectrum, and don't pretend to understand them (if you really don't). Instead, be respectful and use short sentences, speak slowly, or leave large gaps in conversation. Don't try to interrupt any repetitive behaviors (remember, you're not the doctor or therapist). Even though people with autism can have difficulty displaying their emotions, they still have feelings in the same way you do.[10]

21.2 – Discussion Questions

1. How would you describe the three levels of the autism spectrum?
2. What are the key differences between the three levels or the autism spectrum?
3. How should we treat people on the autism spectrum?

21.3 - How to Treat People with Autism

 Greeting teens and young people! It's Dr. Kagan again. Many young people with autism struggle to make friends and may stop trying. And many young people without autism do not get close to someone with autism because they may not understand autism. Sometimes we avoid what we do not understand, without even realizing it. Our initial thoughts and actions are not to engage or reach out to someone who does not reach out to us in the usual ways. But remember what I said earlier. There are so many positives and giving any relationship a chance to work, can open wonderful doors to a great friendship![11] What can you do? Let me suggest some ideas:

If you are living with autism…

- Recognize you are terrific and have wonderful gifts to enjoy and share with others. I read a great book by Dr. Temple Grandin and Richard Panek, The

Autistic Brain-Helping Different Kinds of Minds Succeed that they wrote in 2013. Dr. Grandin tells about growing up with autism, how she struggled and how she recognized her terrific abilities with animals. She became a Doctor in Animal Science. Dr. Grandin is now famous and contributed so much to the world of humane and kind handling of animals. You have greatness in you, as well. It might be hidden from you right now, but eventually you will discover it!

- Do not give up on the social world and making friends. Growing up is not easy for all young people. There is a place for you in that social world. You do not have to be the center of attention, and you do not have to withdraw yourself from the social world. Sometimes it will not work like you hoped. That is okay. Try not to be hard on yourself. Be "you" and be proud of yourself. Keep trying and you will succeed. Pick up some social skills from observing peers and the teaching of professionals who provide social skills training.

- Love and enjoy those things that interest you and you like. Pursue those interests and try some new things. Who knows? Sometimes those interests become the start of an amazing hobby or career that you will love.

If you know someone with autism...

- Try to reach out to that classmate with autism and include them! Have them join your friends' group. Encourage your friends to be friendly and positive. It is not easy for autistic people to make friends. They need your friendship, understanding, sometimes help, and patience. Remember what it was like when you moved to a new school or neighborhood. We all need someone to lean on in times of need. You can be that help!

- Find a shared interest. That always brings people together like video games, music, or a special interest.

- Invite the person with autism to your party or hangout time. Get comfortable interacting with them. Your level of comfort and friendship may be a great example to the other people around you.

Practice the skill of inclusion, and help make this world a better place for all:

- Include... do not socially exclude anyone!

- Be accepting of others!

- Be patient with all people!

- Value yourself and others!

Closing Thought

If you have autism, do not be so hard on yourself. If you know someone with autism, don't be so quick to judge that person; you might make a great friend!

21.3 – Discussion Questions

1. Discuss some positive reasons to have students with Autism Spectrum Disorder more socially included.

2. Whether you are living with Autism Spectrum Disorder or have classmates with such, what can you do to create more inclusion or have students with Autistic Spectrum Disorder more socially included?

Chapter 21 References

[1] "Autism Spectrum Disorder- Symptoms and Causes." Mayo Clinic, 2020, https://www.mayoclinic.org/diseases-conditions/autism-spectrum-disorder/symptoms-causes/syc-20352928.

[2] "Asperger's Syndrome." WebMD, 2020, www.webmd.com/brain/autism/mental-aspergers-syndrome.

[3] American Psychiatric Association. (2013). *Diagnostic and Statistical Manual of Mental Disorders: DSM-5*. https://www.psychiatry.org/psychiatrists/practice/dsm

[4] "Autism Spectrum Disorder." KidsHealth.org, 2020, www.kidshealth.org/en/teens/autism.html.

[5] "Top Ten Positive Traits of Autistic People." Verywell Health, 2020, www.verywellhealth.com/top-terrific-traits-of-autistic-people-260321.

[6] Weitlauf, A. S., Gotham, K. O., Vehorn, A. C., & Warren, Z. E. (2014, February). Brief report: DSM-5 "levels of support:" a comment on discrepant conceptualizations of severity in ASD. https://www.ncbi.nlm.nih.gov/pmc/articles/PMC3989992/.

[7] Rudy, L. (2019, October 01). Making Sense of the 3 Levels of Autism. Retrieved July 21, 2020, from: https://www.verywellhealth.com/what-are-the-three-levels-of-autism-260233.

[8] BS. Abrahams, D., et al., (2017, February 17). An Overview of Autism Spectrum Disorder, Heterogeneity and Treatment Options. Retrieved July 21, 2020, from https://link.springer.com/article/10.1007/s12264-017-0100-y.

[9] Prizant, B. M., &, Fields-Meyer, T. (2019). *Uniquely Human: A Different Way of Seeing Autism.* London: Souvenir Press.

[10] National Council for Behavioral Health. (2016). Mental Health First Aid USA: For Adults Assisting Young People. Washington DC: National Council for Behavioral Health.

[11] Grandin, Temple & Panek, Richard, *The Autistic Brain: Helping Different Kinds of Minds Succeed*, First Mariner Books, 2013.

Chapter 22
LEARNING DISABILITIES

22.1 – What Are Learning Disabilities?

Hey friends, it's Tom again. Learning is a unique experience for all of us. You learn a little differently than your siblings and your friends… and vice versa. Some people are better at math while others prefer English. You may enjoy science while your friend prefers art. Having different interests and abilities is something to be celebrated. **Learning disabilities** (also referred to as **learning disorders** or **alternative abilities**) affect how people perceive information. This can cause issues with how a person learns new information or new skills, but let's be clear: learning disabilities do not affect someone's overall intelligence or motivation. Having a learning disability has nothing to do with how smart someone is or how much they're motivated! Learning disabilities simply affect how people perceive information.[1] Some common symptoms of learning disorders include:

- Struggling to recognize patterns or sorting things in order
- Trouble telling right from left
- Difficulty relaying written information
- Struggling to follow instructions
- Reversing letter or numbers
- Lack of coordination
- Trouble doing things with hands like drawing, cutting, or writing

Like with most disorders, everyone is different and symptoms can be unique to the individual. Learning disorders can cause people to feel frustrated when trying to learn something challenging. This frustration can show itself in the form of anger, sadness, withdrawal, or disruption.

People with learning disabilities often struggle with one or more subjects like reading, writing, and math. They can also have trouble with nonverbal skills like interpreting facial expressions, understanding body language, making eye contact, maintaining attention, and planning ahead.[1]

Learning Disabilities are Permanent Conditions

It's helpful to think of learning disabilities in the same way you might think of learning styles. A learning style is how a person perceives information the most efficiently, and we carry our learning style with us for life. Some people learn by doing rather than listening, others prefer to write down notes or draw. People with learning disabilities simply have a unique learning style.

Learning disabilities are permanent, so we cannot expect a person to be "cured" by going to counseling or taking medications (and besides, that's not our business). However, there are many ways to help people with learning disabilities.

Often, extra help in the classroom is necessary, along with accommodations like extra time for assignments, audiobooks to support reading, and computer software to help with writing and math assignments.[1]

22.1 – Discussion Questions

1. What are some of the common symptoms of learning disabilities?
2. What might someone with a learning disability struggle with outside of class?
3. Why is it helpful to think of people as having different "learning styles?"

22.2 – Common Learning Disabilities

Learning disabilities have many different effects and symptoms, and some are more common than others. Understanding the differences allows us to better relate to ourselves and to the people around us.

In this section we're looking at some of the most common learning disabilities and their effects. Let's start with ADHD.

Attention-Deficit/Hyperactivity Disorder (ADHD)

Attention-deficit/hyperactivity disorder commonly called ADHD is a disorder that causes impulsive actions and exceptionally high level of hyperactivity. ADHD can make it difficult to focus on a single task or sit for long periods of time.[2]

There are several different subtypes of ADHD, but they all portray similar symptoms. Symptoms of ADHD include the following:

- Interrupting people
- Difficulty waiting their turn
- Trouble concentrating
- Fidgeting
- Difficulty sitting still
- Forgetfulness
- Hyperactivity
- Impulsiveness

Although ADHD cannot be cured, it can be treated. Treatment often includes behavioral therapy, talk therapy, medication, or a combination of all three. Managing and understanding symptoms allow people with ADHD to be successful in both academic and personal pursuits.[2]

Dyslexia

Dyslexia is a learning disability that affects the area of the brain that processes language. It involves difficulty reading, writing, and comprehending written information. People with dyslexia tend to mix up letters and sounds when reading and sometimes speaking. Most people with dyslexia have no issues with eyesight, but instead have issues with how words are processed in the brain.[3] Some of the common symptoms of dyslexia include:

- Trouble processing written or spoken information
- Difficulty spelling
- Reading below age level
- Difficulty answering questions or finding the right words to say
- Inability to sound out words
- Trouble seeing and hearing similarities in words or letters
- Taking excessive amounts of time to complete reading or writing tasks
- Avoidance around reading and writing activities

Like other common learning disabilities, dyslexia cannot be cured. Measures can be taken to treat the symptoms of dyslexia. The most common treatment is educational techniques that provide alternatives to traditional reading and writing.

Some techniques include physically tracing letters with fingers, and using vision and touch to better understand language.[4]

Dyscalculia

Dyscalculia is a learning disability that affects math skills and comprehension. It's common for almost everyone to experience some difficulty with math while they're growing up, but having consistent trouble with math while flourishing in other subjects may be a sign of dyscalculia. This condition can make understanding basic math difficult. Things like counting, understanding word problems, or estimating are difficult for people with dyscalculia.[5] Some of the symptoms of dyscalculia include:

- Trouble estimating time or distance

- Trouble learning addition, subtraction, or multiplication

- Trouble understanding fractions

- Difficulties counting money to make change

- Understanding charts or graphs

- Trouble linking a number (5) to its coinciding word (five)

- Difficulty understanding word problems

- Trouble remembering phone numbers

People with dyscalculia cannot be cured, but their experience can be made easier with special teaching plans, math activities, and plenty of practice.

Dysgraphia

Dysgraphia is a nervous system disorder that causes difficulty with fine motor skills like writing. People with dysgraphia have trouble with writing assignments and penmanship. Dysgraphia often shows itself in handwriting, causing distortion, different slants, and a variety of upper and lowercase letters. Dysgraphia also makes it difficult to think and write at the same time, making creative work especially difficult.[6] Some symptoms of dysgraphia include:

- Unfinished or distorted words with missing letters

- Frequent erasing

- Difficulty spacing words and letters on paper

- Irregularly tight grip causing sore hands

- Irregular writing posture

Treatment for dysgraphia depends largely on the individual, but extra support in the classroom and at home can be very effective. Along with this, writing tools like pencil grips, wide-ruled paper, and typing instead of writing can also be helpful (Bhandari, 2018).

Processing Deficits

Processing deficits are caused by the inability to absorb information gathered by the senses. The most common processing deficits are visual and auditory (hearing). This doesn't necessarily mean people with processing issues have trouble seeing or hearing but with comprehending what they see and hear. This can lead to trouble with academics and socialization.

Processing deficit symptoms vary widely depending on which senses are affected and the individual. Some people have trouble recalling things they've heard or seen while others struggle to find where objects or sounds are located in space. Treatment for different processing deficits varies widely, but support in the classroom and at home go a long way.[7]

22.2 – Discussion Questions

1. What are some differences between the common learning disabilities?

2. How can you show dignity to someone with learning disabilities?

3. Cerebral palsy is a condition that affects muscle movement, so it is not a learning disability. Do you think people with cerebral palsy have to face discrimination? Would you speak up if saw someone discriminating? How so?

22.3 – Communicating for Connection

Sometimes people prefer for you to use the term **"alternatively-abled"** instead of **"disabled"** to focus on the positive effects and unique aspects of every human being. If you don't know what someone prefers, you can humbly ask them, and this should not be considered rude as long as you're asking them with a caring heart. Like any other condition or illness, a learning disability does not define you or me. Personally, I have a lot of unique aspects of my life, from severe asthma and allergies to vision issues and mild hearing loss, and if you want to know my preference, I like to be called… Tom. I'd much rather hear my own name rather than "bubble boy." (I hope you see the point here.) When interacting with people who **may have** a disability, it's important to treat them with total equality and dignity. Here are a few pointers:

1. Find What You Have in Common

Before considering someone's learning disability or alternative ability, think about what you have in common. You can find common ground in movies, sports, art, or almost any other subject. As you connect and communicate, you'll start to make a new friend.

2. Be Patient

If you are in a learning environment or any other situation that calls for processing information, be patient. Everyone learns differently, and some people need more time to grasp concepts and directions. Allow them to take their time without feeling rushed or pressured to move on without fully understanding.

3. Don't Assume They See Their Disability as a Weakness

Never assume someone dislikes their learning disability. **Maybe it's simply an alternative ability!**

I'm really being serious here because it's not a joke; it's a reality. And if you're someone living with an alternative ability, that unique aspect of your life can become one of the things you like best about yourself. It really can. Accepting yourself for who you are is key to living a happy and fulfilling life, and we should never assume someone dislikes a piece of themselves. Celebrate everyone for their strengths, and always be supportive.

4. Ask Before Helping

Never assume someone with a learning disability wants extra help from you. If you see a way to be kind or courteous, ask them first if they'd like help, and then ask what works best for them. Everyone likes to feel capable and independent and assuming someone with a learning disability needs help can cause them to feel belittled. Keep an open mind about their capabilities, and don't be afraid to ask if you can support them in some way.

5. Be Kind and Respectful

Above all, be kind and respectful to everyone you meet. We are all uniquely different, and accepting our differences can lead to lifelong friendships and new perspectives. As humans, we all face difficulties in our lives, and connecting with each other makes us feel safe and valued.

22.3 – Discussion Questions

1. Why do some people prefer the term "alternatively-abled?"

2. What are some specific ways to include people with learning disabilities at school and outside of school?

3. Why is it important to ask before helping someone with a learning disability?

Chapter 22 References

[1] Learning Disorders in Children. (2020, July 13). https://www.cdc.gov/ncbddd/childdevelopment/learning-disorder.html.

[2] Angel, T. (2018, November 16). Everything You Need to Know About ADHD. Healthline. https://www.healthline.com/health/adhd#treatment.

[3] Mayo Foundation for Medical Education and Research. (2019, March 12). Learning disorders: Know the signs, how to help. Mayo Clinic. https://www.mayoclinic.org/healthy-lifestyle/childrens-health/in-depth/learning-disorders/art-20046105.

[4] Mayo Foundation for Medical Education and Research. (2017, July 22). Dyslexia. Mayo Clinic. https://www.mayoclinic.org/diseases-conditions/dyslexia/diagnosis-treatment/drc-20353557.

[5] Bhandari, S. (2019, September 5). Dyscalculia: Symptoms & Treatment of the Math Learning Disability. WebMD. https://www.webmd.com/add-adhd/childhood-adhd/dyscalculia-facts.

[6] Bhandari, S. (2018, November 1). Dysgraphia: Signs, Diagnosis, Treatment. WebMD. https://www.webmd.com/add-adhd/childhood-adhd/dysgraphia-facts.

[7] Processing Disorders. Brain Balance. (2019). https://www.brainbalancecenters.com/who-we-help/processing-disorders.

Chapter 23

ADDICTION & SELF-HARM

23.1 – What is Addiction?

Hey y'all! Dr. OH here to give you a quick overview of the technical information about addiction before Tom takes over with a discussion on the impact that addiction can have on you and those around you. The idea of addiction has been the subject of controversy over the years. Some believe that addiction is a choice, and that stepping out of an addiction is as simple as stepping into one. The more current and informed view on addiction understands that addiction is a very complex and personal experience. The DSM-5 refers to **addiction** in the classical sense by using the phrase **substance use disorder**. This separates chemical addictions from behavioral addictions like gambling, or sex. Both kinds of addiction change brain structure and function, but substance abuse causes the greatest brain damage.

4 Symptoms of Addiction

The DSM-5 highlights four categories of symptoms that addicts experience:[1]

1. **Loss of control:** an addict has difficulty controlling how much they use, even when they don't want to use.

2. **Social problems:** an addict lets their personal and professional relationships wither and stops doing the activities they used to care about (unless those activities incorporate the substance).

3. **Unnecessary risk taking:** addicts use in risky situations, including risk of physical harm or death.

4. **Physical dependence:** an addict suffers serious physical symptoms when they don't use enough, which makes successful recovery even more challenging.

Addiction and the Brain

An addict's brain slowly changes to promote and accelerate their addiction. Drugs utilize the functions of neurotransmitters like dopamine, serotonin, and acetylcholine to **activate reward and pleasure centers in the brain** – the same brain areas that are active when you are listening to music you love, eating your favorite food, or after a good exercise session. For the non-addict, this kind of activation is due to a positive sensory experience. For an addict, the activation is due to the drug itself chemically forcing activation. This kind of activation is much stronger, so the brain asks for more and more…and more. Eventually, the brain rewires itself to deal with the intense activity. This rewiring decreases the effect of the drug, and therefore increases the amount of drug necessary for the addict to achieve the same amount of satisfaction.

It's not just the reward networks of the brain that are involved in the substance abuse cycle. Areas involved in decision making, learning, memory, and behavior control have also been found to be physically affected by drug use. Many of these areas are experiencing massive amounts of development in your teenage years, which makes the teenage brain more susceptible to addiction.

Small Group Activity

1. **Instructions:** We have two great websites below that explain a lot more about how addiction affects the brain and your mental health. For this activity we're going to break into groups of three or four people and use a phone or computer to visit either one of the sites below.

2. Each group has five minutes to research the site, and find at least three interesting facts to write down on a notebook. When the five minutes is up, each small group will take a turn presenting their facts to the whole group.

- **Website A – National Institute on Drug Abuse**

    https://www.drugabuse.gov/publications/drugs-brains-behavior-science-addiction/drugs-brain

- **Website B – American Psychiatric Association**

    https://www.psychiatry.org/patients-families/addiction/what-is-addiction

23.2 – How Addiction Lies to You

 I lost a friend to addiction about 10 years ago. His family asked me to speak at his funeral, and I remember barely being able to get through it. We were close enough that I know he would want me to share this with you. Drinking got my friend in legal trouble, and he was required to go to Alcoholics Anonymous meetings regularly and alcohol screenings weekly. He was trying to put his life back together, but ultimately... his addiction destroyed him. The event deeply hurt everyone around him, especially his family. There are no words.

I also want you to know that my life has never has been perfect, and I too have struggled with poor coping mechanisms, so please take these words as a message from both me and from my friend who passed away. I think he would have wanted it that way.

Lie # 1 – The substance is helping you

They say the best lies have a little bit of the truth in them. That's how addiction works. The first lie is that the substance is helpful to you in some way. The substance seems to meet a legitimate need. Maybe it takes the edge off your stress or anxiety. Perhaps it numbs the pain, or it provides some temporary form of pleasure. Psychologists often refer to this as "displacement" – meaning picking a substitute for what you really want or need. The addiction is the substitute for the real thing you desire deep down in your subconscious... which may be more than merely numbing the pain. It could also be seeking something positive in your life like a sense of connection... or fulfillment... or inner peace.

All the while, you're slowly becoming more dependent on something that is definitely harming your brain and may actually destroy your life! You're trying to solve a problem, but you're actually making the problem worse. There's a level of irony to it. The very thing that promises to help you (the substance) is actually slowly destroying you.[2] When you acknowledge this fact, you open your eyes and accept **the truth:** your addiction is ultimately a self-destructive coping skill.[3]

Lie # 2 – You can quit any time

The second lie is that the substance is not a problem, and you can quit any time. People believe this lie very strongly, even when there's proof of how bad the addiction is progressing and demanding more and more from the addict. At this point, the addiction has already re-wired the brain of the user, making them dependent on it. This is why people who abuse drugs or alcohol often experience symptoms of withdrawal when they are forced to stop using.

Lie # 3 – The substance is not affecting your family

The third lie is that the addiction is not hurting anyone else, certainly not the people you love. It's a relationship between the user and the substance only, right? Wrong. As addiction takes hold of a life, the destructive decisions ripple out and cause havoc for everyone, especially family. The truth of addiction is that it increases the risks of mental health problems, domestic violence, financial struggles, physical illnesses, heart attacks, and even death.[4] In a recent study published in August of 2020 by University of California, San Francisco, researchers found that 1 out of every 6 sudden cardiac arrest deaths in San Francisco were connected to drug overdose, especially opioid use.[5] In the United States, 22 million people struggle with drug or alcohol addiction, spending round $600 billion every year on what ultimately amounts to a poor coping skill.[6]

Compassion & Solutions

We need to stop focusing on who's to blame and start having compassion for people who are in recovery, even for those who are still in denial of their addictions. Together, we can be part of their support system by helping them get connected to mental health professionals and addiction treatment centers, so they can break from the bondage of addiction. If you or someone you know is struggling with substance abuse, call the **Substance Abuse National Helpline at 1-800-662-HELP (4357)** or visit **https://www.findtreatment.gov** to find a treatment center near you. Help is available, but you have to take the first step.

23.2 – Discussion Questions

1. In this section, Tom describes three lies surrounding addiction. Can you think of any other ways addiction lies to people?

2. What other tools from this book could help someone address an addiction issue? For example: a strong Support System is proven to help in recovery.

3. Have you ever been directly affected by someone living with addiction? You don't have to share your experience in our group unless you want to. Just remember to contact a trusted adult or contact the phone number above.

23.3 – Self-Harm

Hello again, it's Dr. Kagan. As a school psychologist, I've seen firsthand how self-harm damages the lives of young people, not just physically but also mentally and emotionally… and not just to the person alone, but also to their friends and family. **Self-harm** involves inflicting pain and damage to your own body. It can include cutting, hitting, burning, scratching yourself, and so much more. It's a sign of deep emotional pain, and yes, it can be addicting. Experts believe about **10% of U.S. teens struggle with some form of self-harm.**[7] That's a huge number, and our goal is to help make it smaller.

Self-harm or "non-suicidal self-injury" as it's called by professionals, can be hard to talk about because there's so much shame and stigma around the topic. Sometimes teens feel like "It's my own business and nobody else's!" But please consider our message to you: as trusted adults and mental health professionals, it's our business to try and help you. It is nothing to feel ashamed or embarrassed about. Emotional pain hurts us to the core, and sometimes we resort to anything to make the pain stop.

For those who can't relate to such pain, I am so happy for you. But keep an open mind as you read this, and you may be able to help a friend in serious need.

Like many mental health topics, people used to think that talking about self-harm would only make matters worse and cause more teens to harm themselves. On the contrary, research shows that the more we learn about self-harm (from reliable sources and professionals), and the more we support teens who are suffering, the more we increase their chances of recovery.[8] Take a look at this short quiz, and answer **true** or **false** for each statement:

The reason people self-harm is...

- To take risks. (True or False)

- To be accepted by peers or others. (True or False)

- Out of desperation for attention. (True or False)

- To relieve emotional pain. (True or False)

- To express hopelessness and worthlessness. (True or False)

- Because they have suicidal thoughts. (True or False)

- Because they have serious mental health disorders. (True or False)

- Because they have autism or other developmental disabilities. (True or False)

If you answered "True" for all the statements, you are correct. But there is no single reason that applies to everyone who self-harms. There are even cultures where self-harm is a practiced tradition. Some forms of self-harm are less serious than others. I know teens who try doing their own body piercing or tattooing. This behavior usually has more to do with experimentation and self-expression rather than self-harm (although I still might discourage it because of the health risks involved). The bottom line is, most of the time self-harm indicates a serious problem.

Self-harm is a negative or poor coping skill. That means it lies to your brain, temporarily distracting you or numbing the pain, but destroying you in the process. It can result in scars, infection, isolation, guilt, and lasting shame. Sometimes people harm themselves as a response to trauma in their past, such as physical abuse or sexual abuse. And self-harm can be an expression of more serious mental health problems like depression, bi-polar disorder, suicidal thinking, and more.

Signs of self-harm include frequent unusual cuts, scratches, or marks that are not easily explained. Sometimes the wounds are easy to see, like bruising, burns, or pulled hair. Many times, you don't see it at all because people hide their scars under clothing or bandages. And when asked about their scars, some people give false explanations. Self-harm can include behaviors that are less obvious, such as unhealthy eating and sleeping habits, frequent accidents, and the viewing of photos and websites about self-injury. In any form, the behavior is a physical indication of a deeper mental health problem.

If you or someone you know is struggling with self-harm, you need to get help right away. Even if a friend begs you not to tell anyone, you need to do the right thing and tell a trusted adult, like a parent, guardian, or a mental health worker. If you sense someone is in danger, call 911. You can also call or text the **Lifeline at 988,** and caring people will be there to talk with you, day or night.

The good news is: there is hope and help for people who suffer from self-harm. As we create a safe place to talk about self-harm, it reduces the stigma and improves the chances that people will get help when needed.

23.3 – Discussion Questions

1. Why do you think there is so much stigma and shame around the topic of self-harm?

2. Did you find any of the true or false statements about self-harm to be somewhat surprising? Which ones stuck out to you the most, and why? (Remember, they are all true.)

3. Can you think of other reasons people may harm themselves?

4. What did Dr. Kagan mean when he described self-harm as a "poor or negative coping skill?"

5. If you or a friend was suffering from self-harm, how would you get help?

23.4 – Recovering from Self-Harm

Hey, it's Dr. Kagan again with some practical insights on helping people who suffer from self-harm. If you or a friend is self-harming, you don't have to suffer another day! Take a supportive and non-judgmental look at the problem. **You deserve better!** As a human being, you deserve every chance to enjoy a full life and to recover from the pain that has dominated your very wellbeing. We all must realize that in most self-harm situations, it is an attempt to cope with difficult and painful situations, and we need to show care and compassion for ourselves and for others.

Whatever negative feelings and uncertainty we may have about self-harm, we must put those feelings aside and open our arms, embracing ourselves and others in times of distress. Remember: we gave some solutions about these topics in our chapters on **stigma** and **empathy**.

If you are self-harming, this is your opportunity to face yourself, acknowledge your pain, take responsibility for your actions, and make a promise to get help. It's hard to accept that you actually need help, especially when someone tells you to seek help. At first you might feel angry, resentful, or irritated, but let those feelings turn into appreciation that someone really cares about you.

In all my years as a psychologist, I've seen many success stories, and I believe you can be one too. When you get professional help, such as going to counseling sessions, you can learn how to replace self-harm with more appropriate coping skills. Your counselor or therapist will help you discover which coping skills work best for you.

Let's take a minute to discuss the difference between **non-suicidal self-injury** and **suicide**. In many instances self-harm is not intended to result in death.[9] But it's also true: some people who are engaged in self-harm, do entertain thoughts of suicide. If this is you, go speak with a trusted adult, such as one of your parents or a mental health worker, right away. If you think a friend may be suicidal, ask them directly if they are having suicidal thoughts. Asking such a personal question might seem intimidating at first, but research proves it helps reduce their chances of suicide. Remember, when you ask the question, people don't always give an honest answer. If you're not sure, then contact their parents or a mental health professional immediately. You can also call 911 for emergencies or the National Suicide Prevention Lifeline at 988, which is available 24-hours a day.

Remember, like sailing through stormy weather, life can sometimes be so challenging. But it is also so precious and rewarding as you get through the storm! Some parts of your journey may be very difficult and painful. I humbly don't pretend to fully understand the depths of everyone's struggles. But I want to help you realize that through despair, which is temporary, you can gain enlightenment and gratitude, and have a new appreciation for life. And from that enlightenment you can celebrate and enjoy a life worth living.

23.4 – Discussion Questions

1. How would you respond if you learned a friend was struggling with non-suicidal self-injury?

2. Would you have a different response if the person admitted to having thoughts of suicide? How would you get help?

3. What are some of the important tools you have learned in this section about self-harm?

4. Do you have any other questions about self-harm? You can ask the questions here in this group setting, or if you feel more comfortable, you can ask a trusted adult, like one of your parents or a mental health professional.

5. When you think of the boat metaphor, what are some of the possible positive outcomes that could come by "weathering the storm" of self-harm?

Chapter 23 References

[1] American Psychiatric Association. (2013). *Diagnostic and Statistical Manual of Mental Disorders: DSM-5*. https://www.psychiatry.org/psychiatrists/practice/dsm

[2] Family First Intervention. (2020, January 27). *6 Lies Every Addict Says To Themselves And Their Loved Ones*. Family First Intervention. https://family-intervention.com/blog/6-lies-addict-says-themselves-loved-ones/.

[3] Howard J. Shaffer, P. D. (2017, June 8). What is Addiction? Harvard Health Blog. https://www.health.harvard.edu/blog/what-is-addiction-2017061911870.

[4] National Institute on Drug Abuse. (2020, July 10). *Drugs and the Brain*. National Institute on Drug Abuse. https://www.drugabuse.gov/publications/drugs-brains-behavior-science-addiction/drugs-brain.

[5] Tseng, Z. (2020, August 10). Many Deaths Labeled 'Cardiac Arrest' Could Be Drug ODs: Study. U.S. News & World Report. https://www.usnews.com/news/health-news/articles/2020-08-10/many-deaths-labeled-cardiac-arrest-could-be-drug-ods-study.

[6] https://www.healthypeople.gov/2020/leading-health-indicators/2020-lhi-topics/Substance-Abuse.

[7] Youth Mental Health First Aid USA for Adults Assisting Young People, Maryland Department of Health and Mental Hygiene, Missouri Department of Mental Health, and National Council for Community Behavioral Healthcare, 2012

[8] Self-Harm, Psychology Today, 2020 https://www.psychologytoday.com/us/basics/self-harm.

[9] Understanding Self-Harm/Self-Injury, TeenMentalHealth.org, 2020. https://teenmentalhealth.org/understanding-self-injury-self-harm/.

Chapter 24

RESPONSIBILITY

24.1 – Your Response is Your Responsibility

Greetings teenage human! What does it really take to prove yourself responsible? The answer is more complex than just finishing your homework on time or cleaning up after yourself. **Responsibility is doing what is expected of you and accepting the outcomes of your actions, without making excuses.**[1] The amount of responsibility you need increases as you grow up. When you're born, you have zero responsibilities. You eat. You sleep. You poop. That's all that's expected of you, and rightfully so.

By the time you're a teen, the amount of responsibility required of you is through the roof, so you need to be ready. Responsibility begins with being a **dependable, trustworthy person**. People need to be able to trust that you'll keep your word. They can count on you. What if you don't keep your word? Well, some authority figure in your life will end up holding you accountable. Accountability means being "held to account" for your actions. Ultimately, we all have to own up for the results of our life choices, even our mistakes.

As a teen, when you're faced with a difficult task, it's easy to procrastinate. Every time you put it off, it's still in the back of your head creating anxiety and dread. The more you avoid it, the bigger it gets. But there is a cure for procrastination. The cure is action. The anxiety you feel from procrastinating, immediately disappears once you complete the required task.[2]

Learning the Hard Way

When I was 16, I had a teacher who was famous for getting upset when kids were late for class. He used to point his finger at us and say, **"When you're late, it's like you're saying your time… is more valuable than my time!"** You would think that lesson would stick with me because I heard it so much, but sometimes you have to learn things the hard way. That summer I got my first real job washing dishes at a restaurant called Big Boy. I'm saying "real job" because I already had a weekend paper route, which I kept from age 13 to 18. The interview at Big Boy went great, and they hired me on the spot. I was excited to take another step into adulthood. I guess I really was a big boy since they hired me at Big Boy! They gave me an apron, and told me my first day would be the following Wednesday.

But… when Wednesday rolled around, I completely blanked on my schedule. I remember having this panic moment where I realized I had lost track of time. I jumped up and looked at the clock, realizing I was late for me first day of work! Throwing on my uniform, I got in the car, and drove right over there. I was 12 minutes late, but I clocked in, and went to the back of the restaurant to start training with Glen, the dishwasher man. As he was teaching me how to use the dishwasher, our manager appeared out of nowhere. She asked me to come to the office. My stomach dropped, but I tried to play it cool. I walked into her office, and she asked why I was late on my first day. I just shrugged it off, and said next time I would make sure to call ahead if I was going to be late.

I'll never forget the way she responded. She looked me right in the eyes and said **"If you're going to be late again, don't bother coming in again."** I was stunned. I wanted to make excuses and blame it on other circumstances outside of my control, but something in me paused. It took everything in me to resist the urge to make up an excuse. This really was my fault, 100%, so I calmly apologized to her, and thankfully, she let me get back to work. I knew if I was late again, I would be fired.

From then on, I made a point to arrive at work a few minutes ahead of schedule. That was my way of being extra careful to show myself responsible. I gave myself enough margin, that even if I was running late, I'd still be on time. Sometimes we need to use every trick in the book to make sure we're responsible. And even when we do, we have to acknowledge that we won't always be perfect. Failures are bound to happen.[3]

When we're humble enough to admit our mistakes (rather than make excuses and shift the blame), we start to build back trust and prove we can be responsible.

24.1 – Discussion Questions

1. In your own words, give an example of what it means to be responsible.

2. How is responsibility an important character trait for life?

3. How can admitting our mistakes lead to more trust and responsibility?

24.2 – Locus of Control

 Hey y'all! It's Dr. OH here again. In 1966, a psychologist named Julian B. Rotter from New York coined the phrase *locus of control*.[4] Think locus, as in location and control, as in, well… control. How you handle responsibility in life has a lot to do with your locus of control.

Internal Locus of Control

People with an **internal LOC** feel like they control their own destiny. They are proactive in setting goals and solving problems. They believe that to make things happen, they have to do the hard work.[5]

External Locus of Control

People with an **external LOC** think that everything is controlled by luck, randomness, or other people. These folks don't "own" anything - good or bad.

How do we get our Locus of Control?

According to Dr. Rotter, your locus develops out of your early life experiences with cause and effect. A growing baby spends a lot of time learning that **if** you do one thing, **then** another thing happens. "**If** I cry, **then** adults show up." "**If** I go poddy, **then** my diaper gets changed." As long as the adults provide a stable environment, the kiddo learns what they can and can't control.

When a baby grows up in an unstable environment, they learn cause and effect differently. "If I cry, then adults *may or may not* show up." "If I go poddy, then my diaper *may or may not* get changed." The baby learns that they don't have control over meeting even their most basic of needs.

These kinds of experiences play a part in how your LOC develops throughout your childhood. And because everyone has their own, unique experiences, most people have their own, unique mixture of internal and external locus.[6] That's a good thing! Too much of anything in life is bad (except chocolate). If you *only* operate with an internal locus, you tend to blame yourself for things that aren't your fault. On the other hand, having a completely external outlook means you never see your mistakes, so you never fix them. It can also create anxiety about not having any control over your life.

You're probably thinking, "Hmm. I think I have too much of an in/external locus. Do I control the way I think about control?" Absolutely. Your LOC is a feature of your personality that you can work to improve. But, knowing when to use an internal or external perspective takes practice. Let's have a look at a few hypothetical real-life scenarios:

Accept the things you cannot change.

- Your home gets damaged during a storm.

- Someone close to you dies.

- Your parents get divorced.

Which one of these situations do you have control over? **Not. One**.

You can't control the weather (but that would be a cool superpower). You don't have power over life and death. Your parent's relationship and decisions are theirs, not yours - let them fix their own stuff; you've got enough on your plate.

Change the things you can.

- You barely study and fail an exam.

- You stub your toe on the leg of a table.

- Your parent(s) ground you for breaking the rules.

Which one of these situations do you have control over? **Yep – all of them.**

Instead of failing and saying, "the teacher made the test too hard" say, "I didn't study enough." Instead of stubbing your toe and saying "the universe hates me" say, "I should probably be more careful." Instead of getting grounded and saying, "Ugh! My parents are so mean!" say, "I know the rules, and I shouldn't have broken them without special permission."

Know the difference between what you can and can't change.

You have to be honest with yourself.

If you fail one test and say "the teacher hates me," and then pass another test and say, "I'm so awesome" - you're doing it wrong. If all good things come from you (internal), and all bad things come from not you (external) - you're doing it wrong. You have to know when to take control and set goals, and when to take responsibility and make improvements.

You have to be fair with yourself.

Cut yourself some slack about situations that you can't control. You don't need to carry the weight of the world on your shoulders! If you're having trouble figuring out what is and isn't in your control, an outside point of view can help. Don't be afraid to seek the advice and opinions of others. The important thing is to take control of knowing what you control.

24.2 – Discussion Questions

1. Now that you know a little bit about locus of control, how can you use that knowledge to help you become more responsible?

2. How do you know if you're internal or external? Turns out, Dr. Rotter came up with a handy-dandy scale for measuring that. The activity at the bottom of this section has a few questions from that scale.

   a. Answer these questions on your own first (you don't have to share your answers), then use the key below the questions to see what your answers say about your LOC.

   b. In a group, talk about how each question contributes to understanding a person's LOC. How does each answer option tell you about whether a person is more internal or external?

3. Think about a moment in your life when you should've used an internal perspective instead of an external or vice versa. What could you have done or thought to change your perspective?

Chapter 24 References

[1] Russell, P. (2011, July 27). Moral Sense and the Foundations of Responsibility. https://www.oxfordhandbooks.com/view/10.1093/oxfordhb/9780195399691.001.0001/oxfordhb-9780195399691-e-10.

[2] Terada, Y. (2020, February 11). 3 Reasons Students Procrastinate-and How to Help Them Stop. Retrieved July 02, 2020, from https://www.edutopia.org/article/3-reasons-students-procrastinate-and-how-help-them-stop.

[3] Sussex Publishers. (2019). Perfectionism. Psychology Today. https://www.psychologytoday.com/us/basics/perfectionism.

[4] Rotter, J. B. (1966). Generalized Expectancies for Internal Versus External Control of Reinforcement. Psychological Monographs: General and Applied, 80(1), 1. https://psycnet.apa.org/doi/10.1037/h0092976.

[5] Goolkasian, P. (n.d.). The Locus of Control. University of North Carolina, Charlotte. Retrieved July 15, 2020, from http://www.psych.uncc.edu/pagoolka/LocusofControl-intro.html.

[6] Joelson, R. B. (2017, August 2). Locus of Control. Psychology Today. Retrieved July 15, 2020, from https://www.psychologytoday.com/us/blog/moments-matter/201708/locus-control.

Chapter 25

RESILIENCY

25.1 – 3 Traits of Resilient People

Hey everybody, Tom Thelen here. When you think about a resilient person, what are the first words that pop in your head? People will often describe it as "bouncing back" or "having mental toughness" or "having grit." Those are all good descriptions for resiliency, so the question becomes: how do you get there?

What does it take to become a more resilient person? As humans, we all experience varying degrees of pain, loss and disappointment, so here's what makes resilient people unique: no matter what happens, they find a way to work through the pain, let go of the bitterness over the course of time, and move forward with their lives. Their past pain doesn't determine their future. It doesn't "own them" anymore.

And let me tell you, it's NOT an easy process… especially if you've been hurt or betrayed by someone close. But man is it worth it. You're worth it, and that's the truth. Resiliency doesn't always come natural to us. It's a skill you work on over time until it becomes part of who you are. Here are three common traits of resilient people:

1. Resilient people focus on what they can control.

Resilient people have an **internal locus of control**, which means they believe they have control over their own life. (Dr. OH just talked about that in the previous chapter!) They understand that their choices are like the steering wheel of the ship, controlling the direction and major outcomes of their life. Resilient people focus on what they can influence and what they can change, and then they let go of the things they can't control.[1]

2. Resilient people are proactive problem-solvers.

When you're resilient, you see challenges as opportunities. When there is a problem, you don't give up. You come up with creative solutions.[2] Think about the challenges to your social life during the Coronavirus pandemic. Some students slipped into social isolation and even depression, while others got proactive and found ways to stay connected digitally. That's being a proactive problem solver.

3. Resilient people have a strong support system.

Resilient people don't try to tackle problems alone, and they aren't afraid to ask for help. They share their emotions and listen to feedback from people in their "inner circle," (aka: their support system). When they're feeling weak or hurt or alone or sad, they contact the people in their support system and open up about what's really going on in their lives. That's their secret source of strength.[3]

Malala Yousafzai: The Teen Who Changed the World

In 2008 an 11-year-old girl in Pakistan named Malala Yousafzai wrote in her diary about her life living under the laws of a military group called the Taliban. The Taliban had taken over as the new government in her country, and they were known for their inhumane treatment of women and girls. Under Taliban law, girls were not even allowed to attend school. Did you catch that…? ALL GIRLS were being denied an education. Malala published the diary on a BBC blog without putting her name on it, so she could be anonymous. Her first post was titled, "I am afraid." It immediately became popular, and millions of people read her story.[4]

Eventually Malala got the courage to reveal she was the author of the diary. And then she took it one step further. She started sharing her views in person… in public settings. Malala knew she was putting her own life at risk by speaking up against the Taliban, but she did it anyway.

She shared her views on equal rights for women and the importance of education for all girls. Fair treatment under the law was her core message (something everyone should agree with, right?), but the Taliban leaders started saying she should be silenced for spreading dangerous beliefs.

Over the next three years, Malala faced public ridicule, and some people even threatened to hurt her and her family. In the face of all that pressure, she continued to speak up and spread her positive message of hope.

Then, one day Malala's life changed forever. Without warning, a gunman came on her school bus and shot her in the head. Miraculously, she survived the shooting and was able to recover over time.

Malala Yousafzai would let nothing stop her – not even a gun. In fact, after recovering she became even more committed to the cause of education for women and girls, and her message started reaching a worldwide audience.

Malala Yousafzai

In 2014, Malala became **the youngest person in history** to win the Nobel Peace Prize – an international award usually given to older politicians and world leaders. Clearly, Malala was becoming a leader and making a huge impact on the world. During her acceptance speech she said:

"This award is not just for me. It is for those forgotten children who want education. It is for those frightened children who want peace. It is for those voiceless children who want change. I am here to stand up for their rights, to raise their voice."[5] **– Malala Yousafzai**

Today, Malala is an activist for female education, and she continues to inspire people around the world. When many people would have given up, Malala bounced back. That, my friends, is true grit. That is resiliency.

25.1 – Discussion Questions

1. Using the 3 Traits of Resilient People, list three examples of how Malala Yousafzai was resilient in her life.

2. What are some situations in life where it's hard to be resilient and "bounce back" from something hurtful?

3. Can you think of more examples of young people who displayed resiliency in their lives? List a few examples, and discuss how they were resilient.

4. Describe one situation in your own life that was challenging, but you bounced back from it.

25.2 – Becoming More Resilient

What's up! It's Dr. Kirleen here to talk about resilience! Picture this: a marathon runner trains for years to run the race of a lifetime. She is within minutes of winning the race when suddenly she's overcome by exhaustion and falls down, collapsing to the ground. Despite seeing her dreams crushed right in front of her eyes, she finds the will to crawl to the finish line. It's a true story. **Hyvon Ngetich**, an elite marathon runner from Kenya had the unfortunate fate of having this very experience during the 2015 Austin Marathon. When asked why she kept going, she said, **"Running … you always have to keep going and going."**[6] You've probably never crawled to the finish line of a race, but I want you to know you are resilient. Every time you've kept going when you felt like stopping something hard or difficult, you were showing the same grit as Hyvon Ngetich. Building resiliency is a fundamental step in getting through your teenage years and becoming a successful adult. In life, resilient people still get exhausted just like everyone else, and sometimes they even fall, but they always dig down deep and find the strength to finish the race.

Bounce Back Power

As Tom described in the previous section, resiliency is the ability to "bounce back" from difficult circumstances and demanding situations. Being resilient means managing any leaks in your boat. To bounce back from adversity, you have to tap into your resiliency skills. Resiliency is a life skill that can be learned over time, but you have to be intentional about it.[7]

You've Got "Bounce Back Power" If…

- If you're aware of your emotions and try to deal with them in a healthy way

- If you try to stay away from acting or thinking impulsively

- If you try to have an optimistic outlook on most days

- If you try to think through situations in a flexible and accurate way

- If you show empathy toward others
- If you believe you can achieve great things
- If you are willing to seek help when needed

5 Skills for Bouncing Back (Resiliency)

1. Practice having healthy beliefs about yourself.

A harmful opinion about yourself can range from not feeling attractive enough, rich enough, popular enough, or feeling like you aren't enough in general. Everything takes energy (like all boats take fuel), including the thoughts you have. Mentally healthy people don't waste energy on limiting thought patterns. Instead, they focus their energy on bettering their situation and leveling up in life. This looks like trying new things (even if you're afraid you might fail), being kind to yourself, and thinking about your strengths.

2. Deal with the elephant in the room.

Mentally resilient people don't ignore the elephant in the room - meaning they don't ignore their problems, but instead face them head-on.[8] For example, if you've been struggling to get along with your best friend but choose to ignore the issue, nothing will get fixed. You will continue to cycle through the negative relationship until you decide to face the problem and talk about your feelings with your friend. Resilient people take their issues in stride and see problems or failures as an opportunity to learn. They acknowledge the problem and fully commit to fixing it before it gets out of hand.

3. Know how your backstory affects your today story.

No one is perfect. We all come to the table with something. Understanding how events from your history affect your behaviors and actions today is vital in building resiliency. It's easy to be reactive to triggers you've learned throughout childhood. Emotional triggers can lead you to have anger outbursts, shut down, or people-please to be liked. But ultimately, these behaviors are self-defeating and they hurt your relationships. Resilient people understand how their past impacts their present, but they don't let it determine their future. They have too much self-respect and self-esteem to stay stuck in the past or to be defined by it.

4. Cultivate balanced relationships.

Unbalanced relationships can happen in friendships, with family members, or even with a romantic partner. When a relationship is unbalanced, one person is doing most of the giving while the other is doing most of the taking. It's not reciprocal. If you feel mentally drained after spending time with someone, take a look at the effort ratio. Who is giving more to the relationship, and how does that make you feel? Having negative beliefs about yourself can lead to staying in relationships where you aren't valued. Resilient people make a significant effort to surround themselves with those who make them feel inspired, happy, and fulfilled. They find balance in their relationships.

5. Recognize thinking traps.

Mentally resilient people don't participate in thinking traps. Thinking traps, also called cognitive distortions, are habitual ways of thinking that are often inaccurate and negatively biased. You can fall into a thinking trap by merely comparing yourself to others or dwelling on the negative. If one bad thing happens in a sea of good things, and you choose to react to the bad, then you're falling into a thinking trap. Negative self-beliefs can be damaging to your life progression, especially if you fall into these patterns often. You have to press the mental reset button and learn to snap out of it. Your thoughts should inspire you to greatness instead of bringing you down or holding you back. **Below are three of the most common thinking traps:**

- **Jumping to Conclusions** – Making irrational assumptions about people or about circumstances. "I know they meant that text in a mean way."

- **Catastrophizing** – Blowing circumstances out of proportion. Every setback feels like a huge catastrophe! "My life is ruined!"

- **Personalization** – Consistently taking the blame for everything that goes wrong with our life. "It must be my fault."

You Are Resilient

Think about the boat metaphor. Life doesn't come with a step-by-step map, and that's okay. Resilient people use what they have on hand, everything under their power to guide their boat. They use the compass, the periscope, and lighthouses to steer their choices toward a meaningful direction. They manage the aspects of life they can control, and they let go of what they can't control. Resilient boats still have to navigate through big waves and stormy weather from time to time, but they get through it and they keep going.

We all experience twists and turns in life, from everyday challenges to traumatic events with lasting impacts. Resiliency gives you **bounce back power** to never give up. Even when you fall down, you always get back up and finish the race. That makes you resilient.

25.2 – Discussion Questions

1. What does it mean to be resilient and how can you learn to be more resilient?

2. Review the 5 skills to building resiliency discussed in this section and categorize them in order of most to least important to you and discuss why? Base your answer on your personal opinion.

3. Share a time when you were NOT resilient and discuss how you could have used resiliency skills to be more successful.

Chapter 25 References

[1] Munoz, R. T., Brady, S., & Brown, V. (2017). The Psychology of Resilience: A Model of The Relationship of Locus of Control to Hope Among Survivors of Intimate Partner Violence. Traumatology. https://doi.apa.org/doiLanding?doi=10.1037%2Ftrm0000102.

[2] Pinar, S. E., Yildirim, G., & Sayin, N. (2018, May). Investigating the Psychological Resilience, Self-Confidence and Problem-Solving Skills of Midwife Candidates. Nurse Education Today. https://www.sciencedirect.com/science/article/abs/pii/S0260691718300807?via%3Dihub.

[3] Ottilingam Somasundaram, R., & Devamani, K. A. (2016). A Comparative Study on Resilience, Perceived Social Support and Hopelessness Among Cancer Patients Treated with Curative and Palliative Care. Indian Journal of Palliative Care. http://www.jpalliativecare.com/article.asp?issn=0973-1075;year=2016;volume=22;issue=2;spage=135;epage=140;aulast=Somasundaram.

[4] The Nobel Prize (2014). Malala Yousafzai Biographical. The Nobel Foundation by Science History Publications. https://www.nobelprize.org/prizes/peace/2014/yousafzai/biographical/.

[5] Wikipedia.org. Retrieved from https://en.wikipedia.org/wiki/Malala_Yousafzai.

[6] Reduced to Her Knees, Marathoner Finishes Race in A Crawl. (2015). Retrieved October 13, 2020. https://www.npr.org/sections/thetwo-way/2015/02/17/386983481/reduced-to-her-knees-marathoner-finishes-race-in-a-crawl.

[7] Teach your Teenager to be Resilient. https://parents.au.reachout.com/skills-to-build/wellbeing/things-to-try-coping-skills-and-resilience/teach-your-teenager-to-be-resilient.

[8] Building Your Resilience. (2012). https://www.apa.org/topics/resilience.

Chapter 26

BECOMING YOUR BEST SELF

26.1 – Active Listening

Hey everybody, it's Tom again. This last chapter is PACKED with practical steps for improving your mental health and wellbeing. It starts with using our number one tool for building healthy relationships: **Active Listening**. No one is born an active listener. As babies, we listen when we're curious or when we want something. Some people never outgrow this default approach to listening. **Active listening means listening to understand.** Much of active listening is about showing the other person you value them enough to be the kind of listener they need in that moment.[1]

I'm sure you know people who only listen until they can jump in and give their own advice and opinions. They just need to talk. It becomes clear very quickly – they're not really listening! If you struggle with this, here's how to spot it in yourself: if the other person is talking and you're only thinking about what you're about to say, then you're not really listening. You're simply preparing your next speech. Or what about the distracted listener? Nothing kills a good conversation like a distracted listener. Let's face it: if you're talking to someone and they start to check their phone, or maybe they start looking off in the distance, you'll get the message loud and clear. They're not even present. They're somewhere else.

To be an active listener is so much more engaging. It starts with having a genuine desire to understand the other person. Think of the attitude you have when you're listening to someone who really interests you. You're showing them that you're engaged with your body language, the words you use, and your tone of voice… when you wait for your turn to respond. Your attitude gives the other person social cues indicating, "I'm here, and I'm listening because what you're saying is important to me."

Make eye contact with the other person, but try not to stare at them. Experts say you should maintain eye contact for about **70% of the time while listening**. It shows you're interested and attentive. And side note: you only need to make eye contact about **50% of the time while talking**.[2]

Now this is key: to really develop the skill of active listening, you have to take it one step further and **check for understanding**. You need to make sure you're both on the same page. You can say something like, "So what I'm hearing you say is (and then paraphrase or summarize what you think they said) …is that right?" A lot of times the other person will gladly circle back to clarify what they meant, or they'll say something like, "Yes, that's it, and you know what else…" At that point they can open up, and you'll continue to grow a trusting relationship.[3]

8 Active Listening Skills

You're ready to listen. Your attitude is open, respectful, and caring. You genuinely want to understand what the other person is trying to say. So how do you practice active listening? Follow these eight tips:

1. **Check for understanding.** See if you're on the same page by paraphrasing what you just heard with a question like, "So what I hear you saying is (and then paraphrase what you think they're saying)… is that right?"

2. **Summarize.** Sum it all up to show you understand what you just heard. Be careful not to oversimplify their message, and don't rush it.

3. **Show that you're listening.** Maintain eye-contact for about 70% of the time while listening (and 50% while talking). Give brief, encouraging responses, and use friendly and attentive body language. And of course, don't mess with your phone.

4. **Empathize with them.** Let the other person know you're aware of their feelings. You can say something like, "I can see why you'd be angry."

5. **Give feedback.** Answer questions, make observations, and share relevant information and experiences. Just remember to spend more time listening than talking.

6. **Ask thoughtful questions.** Good questions can help draw the speaker out of their shell, and they show that you really want to understand.

7. **Validate them.** Respond in a way that shows support. For example, "I know this isn't easy talk about. Thank you for being open with me."

8. **Know when to zip it.** Sometimes, the best thing to do is stay quiet and listen with a caring heart. Sometimes people just need to be heard, and they aren't looking for a solution (just ask my wife).

7 Bad Habits to Break

Now that you know **what to do**, let's look at **what not to do.**

1. **Don't interrupt.** When you feel the urge to interrupt… and we all do sometimes… try to hold back and really listen, even if you're afraid you might forget what you're about to say. Let the thought go and return to listening. (If what you were gonna say was that important, you'll remember it later.)

2. **Don't simply ask "Why?"** Even if you wait for your turn to speak, this feels like an interruption – or an interrogation. It can put people on the defensive.

3. **Don't be too reassuring.** When someone rushes to reassure you ("Oh, there's no reason to be angry!"), it feels dismissive and invalidating.

4. **Don't be too quick to offer advice.** This one feels dismissive and condescending. It's better to actively listen and then ask good questions, letting the other person come to their own conclusion. If they ask for your advice, give it.

5. **Don't pry.** You don't need to know everything – some things are not your business. Don't try to dig too deep if you can tell the other person is getting uncomfortable.

6. **Don't preach.** Avoid saying "You should…" or "You shouldn't…" Let the other person say what they need to say without feeling judged or criticized.

7. **Don't patronize.** Avoid saying things like "You poor thing! I know just how you feel!" People don't need your pity or sympathy. They need a caring friend with a listening ear.

6 Benefits of Active Listening

As you develop the skill of active listening, it will improve your relationships and help you become the person you want to be. Take a look. The benefits are huge!

1. People will talk to you because you've earned their trust.

2. You'll have more friends and deeper relationships.

3. You'll develop more empathy and compassion for others and for yourself.

4. You'll gain a deeper appreciation for different points of view.

5. You'll retain more information and maybe even do better in school.

6. You'll develop a better understanding of yourself and the people around you.

Those are a lot of great benefits! I want to challenge you to make active listening something you do automatically, without even thinking about it. That means you'll have to intentionally practice until it becomes a habit.

Active listening is a vital skill you can start developing now and continue building the rest of your life. It's proof that you're fully present and in the moment. It will help you make more friends and have deeper conversations because it shows people that you really care.

26.1 – Discussion Questions

1. How can you tell when someone is actively listening to you? What are some ways they show that they're really listening?

2. What does it feel like when you're having a conversation with someone, and they start looking down at their phone? Or maybe they stop making eye contact with you... how does that feel? What kind of messages are they sending?

3. Here's a situation: One of your best friends starts to open up and talk with you. They're going through something that is very difficult for them to talk about. Meanwhile, you can't help it... your phone is buzzing in your pocket. You keep getting notifications. What do you do?

4. What are some other responses or mannerisms we should try to avoid while listening?

5. What are some situations where it is difficult to be an active listener?

26.2 – Set Big Goals for Your Life

So... here we are! The last section of the book! I hope you feel equipped with the tools to navigate your "boat" through the obstacles, opportunities, and challenges of life. And yet, there's always room to grow. That's why it's so important to set goals. People who set personal goals are more prepared to see future possibilities, and to make them into a reality.

Research shows that goal setters are more confident, motivated, and independent in life.[4] They're more resourceful. They take measured risks to solve problems and shape the future.

By setting big goals for your life, you're accepting responsibility as the captain of your own ship. Think about the boat metaphor from chapter 2. You're looking through the periscope, checking the compass, and steering toward a specific life direction.

How Do You Define Success and Failure?

The human experience always includes both success and failure. How you define each term shapes your identity. Remember in chapter 3 we talked about how **perfectionism destroys self-esteem?** That happens when you start to define yourself by your successes and failures. The terms "success" and "failure" define events and endeavors - not people. You are either successful at accomplishing a goal, or you fail at accomplishing a goal.[5]

Failing at something doesn't make you a "failure" because events and endeavors don't define you. That is so important to your mental health. If you're tying your self-worth to your accomplishments, tell yourself to knock it off. Not cool.

What if you could flip it around in your head? What if you started seeing mistakes and failures as necessary steps toward success? Each mistake can teach you something new, as long as you don't tie your self-worth to it.

Did you know in Major League Baseball, the best batters only get a hit around 30% of the time? Do you think they consider themselves failures the other 70% of the time? Of course not! They know the more chances they take, the more hits they'll get. Life is like that.

The only thing is: we don't have to wait in line for our turn to bat. We have unlimited at-bats… new chances to succeed or fail every day, and yet we let our fear of failure (meaning our perfectionism) scare us away for stepping up to the plate and swinging for the fences.

As you learn to take your mistakes in-stride, you can be more comfortable in your own skin. Heck, you can even laugh at yourself when you fail. When you refuse to be defined by success or failure, you can drop the perfection, and give yourself permission to try again.

Brainstorm About Your Future

Coming up with a goal is pretty easy, but actually achieving it can be pretty difficult. Goal "stick-with-it-ness" (not exactly a scientific term) becomes much more likely if you follow these three steps:

1. **Dream big – realistically:** Think of where you want to go and who you want to be, but think about it in bite-size chunks. If you want to improve your physical health, don't immediately jump to running a marathon. Work toward your goal one step at a time.

   Set a realistic training schedule. Start by running a mile (or even a quarter mile or a half-mile) three times a week and work up from there. Ask your gym teacher to help you create a safe and challenging training schedule.

2. **Trust your gut:** You want a goal to be something that has true meaning and value to you. Do it for yourself, not for your parents or anyone else. Dig deep and choose something you'd truly like to become or achieve

3. **Finally, write it down.** Remember the old saying: a goal is only a dream until you write it down. There's actually plenty of research proving why that's true! For some reason, when we put the pen to paper (or fingers to a keypad), goal setting becomes concrete and your chances of achieving them go through the roof. To make things a little easier, make use of the widely known acronym **SMART**, which works to help you create goals that are **Specific, Measurable, Achievable, Realistic,** and **Time-Bound**.[6]

What are SMART Goals?

Setting SMART Goals is a way of simplifying the goal-setting process. But let's be honest—you still have to do the work—and that means using some of that handy-dandy prefrontal cortex of yours. Get to it!

Specific: What exactly do you want to achieve? A good goal will be clear and defined. For example, if you are interested in being more mindful, instead of writing, "I want to be more mindful," you might write, "I will practice deep breathing for 10 minutes every night before I go to bed."

Measurable: How will you check your progress? You want to be able to track how much you're improving – daily, weekly and monthly. With the example above, you might write, "I will log my mindfulness every night that I meditate." You can keep track on your phone or go old school and print out a blank monthly calendar, so you can mark a big **X** for every day you make progress.

Achievable: What are the steps you need to take to reach the goal? It takes a bit of brainstorming. Writing out your SMART goals isn't always linear. When you first decide that you'd like to be more mindful (still using the example above), you could write out several ways to reach your goal. You should even write down the very first steps toward achieving the goal, like "Add a daily alarm on my phone." that reminds me to take a deep breath and to look at my feet." Write as many ideas as you can. It doesn't have to be perfect, and you can edit it down later once your path to the goal becomes clearer.

Relevant: Why is this goal important to you? Does this goal define who you want to be and where you want to go? Does it help create a better future for you? This is also part of the brainstorming process. If you choose that you'd like to be more mindful, perhaps it's because you've been feeling stressed out. The goal has to be really important to you, or you won't have the motivation to follow through.

Time-Bound: When do you want to achieve this goal? Set a target date as a guide toward your goal. To wrap up our example, you might write, "I will set a reminder for one month from now, so I can evaluate my progress and decide whether to increase my time or begin working on another mindfulness goal."

I really do believe you already have what it takes to become an amazing, well-rounded, mentally healthy person. Sure, you still have things to work on in your life (we all do), but that's what makes the growth process to beautiful.

26.2 – SMART Goal Activity

1. Think about where you want to be one month or a year from now. What does your life look like? How will you be more mentally healthy?

2. Think about one specific SMART goal you want to achieve as a result of reading this book, and write the details in your phone. Make a calendar reminder revisit the goal monthly and check on your progress. You got this!

My SMART Goals

- Specific –

- Measurable –

- Achievable –

- Relevant –

- Time-Bound –

Chapter 26 References

[1] Grande, D. (2020, June 2). Active Listening Skills: Why Active Listening is Important, and How to Do It. Psychology Today. Retrieved July 28, 2020 from https://www.psychologytoday.com/us/blog/in-it-together/202006/active-listening-skills.

[2] Schulz, J. (2018, October 2). Eye Contact: Don't Make These Mistakes. Michigan State University Extension. www.canr.msu.edu/news/eye_contact_dont_make_these_mistakes.

[3] Grohol, J.M. (2020, May 20). Become a Better Listener: Active Listening. Psych Central. https://psychcentral.com/lib/become-a-better-listener-active-listening/.

[4] Price-Mitchell, M. (2018, March 14). "Goal-Setting Is Linked to Higher Achievement." Psychology Today. https://www.psychologytoday.com/us/blog/the-moment-youth/201803/goal-setting-is-linked-higher-achievement.

[5] Sharma, M. (2015). Your Definition of Success and Failure Impact Your Child. White Swan Foundation. www.whiteswanfoundation.org/life-stages/childhood/your-definition-of-success-and-failure-impacts-your-child-do-you-know-your-definition.

[6] "Goal Setting for Teens" Teen SMART Goals. (2020, April 30). https://www.teensmartgoals.com/goal-setting-for-teens.

The Thelen Family
From left to right: Ellie, Jack, Casie, Tom, Addie (holding Willie), & Lucy

"Your life will be as great as you make it be or as small as you let it be."

- Tom Thelen

Connect With Us!

https://MentalHealth101.org – Discover our award-winning school curriculum.

https://ResetSchools.org – Partner with our mental health nonprofit.

https://TomThelen.com – Book a live speaking event with Tom Thelen.

https://NeelyCounseling.com – Learn about Dr. Kirleen's counseling center.

https://KimDoesResearch.com – Learn about Dr. OH's research and writing.

https://NoBullyingSchools.com – Use our bullying prevention software & app.

My Notes

The remaining pages are left blank for you to add your own notes and ideas!

Made in United States
North Haven, CT
21 September 2023

41808629R00120